THE *Journey* TO SONSHIP

POSSESSING YOUR INHERITANCE

Lydia Newton

Copyright © 2009 - Lydia Newton

All rights reserved. This book is protected under the copyright laws. This book may not be copied or reprinted for commercial gain or profit. The use of short quotations or occasional page copying for personal or group study is permitted and encouraged. Permission will be granted upon request. Unless otherwise identified, Scripture quotations are taken from the Holy Bible, New International Version®. Copyright © 1973, 1978, 1984 by International Bible Society. Used by permission of Zondervan Publishing House. Scripture quotations marked NKJV are taken from the New King James Version, Copyright © 1982 by Thomas Nelson Publishers, Inc. Used by permission. All rights reserved. Scripture quotations marked AMP are taken from the Amplified® Bible, Copyright © 1954, 1958, 1962, 1964, 1965, 1987 by The Lockman Foundation. Used by permission. All rights reserved. Scripture quotations marked Literal Translation are taken from the Interlinear Bible version used: English translations: Holy Bible: New International Version®. Copyright 1973, 1978, 1984 by International Bible Society. Used by permission of Zondervan Publishing House. Emphasis within Scripture quotations is the author's own. Please note that Destiny Image Europe's publishing style capitalizes certain pronouns in Scripture that refer to the Father, Son, and Holy Spirit, and may differ from some Bible publishers' styles.

Take note that the name satan and related names are not capitalized. We choose not to acknowledge him, even to the point of violating grammatical rules.

DESTINY IMAGE™ EUROPE srl
Via Maiella, 1
66020 San Giovanni Teatino (Ch) - Italy

"Changing the world, one book at a time."

This book and all other Destiny Image™ Europe books are available at Christian bookstores and distributors worldwide.

To order products, or for any other correspondence:

DESTINY IMAGE™ EUROPE srl
Via Acquacorrente, 6
65123 - Pescara - Italy
Tel: +39 085 4716523 - Fax: +39 085 9431270
E-mail: info@eurodestinyimage.com
Or reach us on the Internet: **www.eurodestinyimage.com**

ISBN: 978-88-89127-77-3
For Worldwide Distribution, Printed in the U.S.A.
1 2 3 4 5 6 7 8/13 12 11 10 09

Dedication

I dedicate this book to the precious Holy Spirit, who has been my "keeping power" during my years of formation and growing up into sonship.

I also dedicate it to all believers who are being called to a place of complete surrender to the formation process and who are bewildered at the form the journey is taking.

Acknowledgments

I want to say a special thank you to Mrs. Pauline Rawlins for teaching me a very valuable lesson, "God is always present whether I feel Him or not."

Thank you also to my darling husband for being a strong tower during the crucial stages of my formation process and to all those who made the journey together with me. I'm looking forward to the next dimension of the exploration of the heart of Abba.

And I extend my appreciation to Jacqueline Newton for her patience and commitment in editing this work.

Endorsements

I wish you many congratulations on your second book, *The Journey to Sonship*. I have read the book thoroughly, and it was indeed a blessing to me. I found it to be quite inspirational. Your knowledge of Scripture is evident, and I'm sure this work will be a motivational tool for all who are privileged to read it. Because we are living in the end times, the material in your book is vital to the Kingdom of God for such a time as this.

Keep on writing books and encouraging the people of God to be effective in this earthly realm. May the grace and peace of God be with you.

Bishop Sylvester Banks, Sr.
Bible Church of God, Inc.

The Journey to Sonship is for those who desire a deeper walk with Christ and those who want to access the fullness of what God has prepared for His children from the foundations of the earth. It is clear that Lydia has poured her own personal experiences into this book. She has an earnest desire that what has captured her and motivated her may be found and experienced by others, specifically those who are coming into the Shalom of God, where there is nothing missing or broken and our commitment will be to a surrendered will that whispers, "Be it unto me according to Your Word."

Throughout *The Journey to Sonship*, the believer is encouraged to a change in configuration from distorted, ungodly beliefs of past experiences. The author asserts that our makeup must be changed so that our constitution (the rules and laws we are governed by) can come into full agreement with the heartbeat of Heaven written in the Word of God.

Adrian Agard
CEO, Things Gospel and Gospel Connection
Bridgetown, Barbados

"Come and eat the meat… and come into the fullness of God." As I read, this is the cry throughout these pages. The author took the time to walk us through our inheritance in God, taking us from God sending us forth from His mouth, to being impregnated in our mother's womb, being born in the earth, being saved (our born-again experience) and walking in our full purpose according to His plan for each one of us. As we journey through our paths—whether trials, troubles, or successes—they end with us walking as sons of God in the earth, knowing fully who we are and whose we are. Thank you, Lydia, for allowing us to journey with you.

Beverley Walters
Manager, Wealth Management
Bridgetown, Barbados

Table of Contents

Foreword 11
Preface 15
Introduction. 19

Section I
The Success of the Journey Guaranteed Through Covenant Promise

Introduction. 23

Chapter 1	Embrace Your Birthright 25
Chapter 2	The Interpretation of the Promise and Covenant. . 33
Chapter 3	The Lord Will Do Anything to Protect the Promise 39
Chapter 4	No Covenant Without a Sacrifice, No Sacrifice Without an Altar 43

Section II
The Deception of Mistaken Identity

Introduction. 53

Chapter 5	Who I Am… Is *in* the I AM!.	55
Chapter 6	The Assignment	61
Chapter 7	Hindrances to Accessing the God Within	65
Chapter 8	The Battle Begins – Part 1	71
Chapter 9	The Battle Begins – Part 2, The Victory Won	79
Chapter 10	The Battle Rages – Part 1	81
Chapter 11	The Battle Rages – Part 2, Our Triune Being	87
Chapter 12	The Regulations of the Temple	93

Section III
The Process of the Journey

	Introduction	101
Chapter 13	God Chastens Those He Loves	109
Chapter 14	It Is Time to Be Healed	113
Chapter 15	Time to Possess	119

Section IV
Encounters on the Journey

	Introduction	129
Chapter 16	Christ's Physical Corporate Body	131
Chapter 17	The Mystery of the Communion	135
Chapter 18	The Marketplace	145
Chapter 19	Our Role and Assignment in the Marketplace	151
Chapter 20	Understanding Our Sphere of Authority in the Marketplace	155
Chapter 21	Know What Controls the Area of Your Assignment in the Marketplace	163
	From My Heart to Yours	171

Foreword

Ever so often God directs us to a work containing the right ingredients that encapsulates in a finished product the understanding of the mystery of God's plan for His prized possession—His children.

From Genesis to Revelation, we sometimes get lost while attempting to capture the fullness of God's purpose for our lives. As we grapple to bring together all the pieces that confront us from the moment of our entrance into the Kingdom through our salvation experience, we are left with an incomplete tapestry of God's masterpiece. With so much information available to us through books, manuals, brochures, seminars, conferences, sermons, sermonettes, preachers, teachers, televangelists, and the lot, we find ourselves stuck in a labyrinth of knowledge that serves more to test our retentive capabilities than to bring us into a knowledge of the truth.

Some of us exist under a cloud of such vast choices that our discernment to recognize truth becomes impaired. We confuse process for punishment, age for maturity, subservience for honor, material possessions for blessings, Scripture regurgitation for substance, community for unity, and worldly influence for favor. Our impressions of Kingdom living are diluted to the extent that the substance of God's

Preface

In all your getting, get understanding (Proverbs 4:7).

As we journey on our pathway to sonship, one of our greatest and most valuable discoveries will be to understand the ways of God. Without that understanding, we will become disappointed on the journey.

We read in Romans 11:33 (NKJV), *"Oh, the depth of the riches both of the wisdom and knowledge of God! How unsearchable are His judgments and His ways past finding out!"* With this in mind, we also see the wisdom of Father in giving us the precious Holy Spirit, who Jesus said will lead us into all truth and reveal these unsearchable mysteries of God. The Holy Spirit will unveil the mysteries of the ways of God to us as we submit ourselves to the *Word* becoming flesh within us. God has poured Himself out on the pages of His Word so that we can have at least a glimpse of His ways. To know His ways is to know His heart, and His heart speaks loudly and in some cases painfully in His Word.

SECTION I

The Success of the Journey Guaranteed Through Covenant Promise

*"It is finished;
it will always be finished."*

Introduction

At the onset of this book, I would like to draw the believer into a legal discourse that the enemy for centuries has argued using the believer's past experience and a misinterpretation of the *love* of God and the process of the journey. This discourse is the primary hindrance to full possession of his or her right to the inheritance given by the Father and signed with the blood of the Lamb—Jesus Christ Himself.

The "accuser of the brethren" is a true description of the method the enemy has always used and continues to use to defraud the believer of his/her birthright. This section will introduce and in many cases reintroduce the believer to the truth that lies within the pages of the Word of God. Acknowledging, accepting, partaking, and possessing the truth will place the believer in his/her position as a son—one who is endowed with the power to defy and denounce the lies and mirages that have been created in the mind, and refuses to be denied his/her right to be anything other than a possessor of God.

Chapter 1

Embrace Your Birthright

So Esau despised his birthright (Genesis 25:34).

WHAT HAVE WE DONE WITH OUR BIRTHRIGHT?

The issue of birthright is very important to God. Throughout the history of the Church as early as the community of Israel, God impressed upon His people the importance of the birthright.

The word *birthright* speaks of the inheritance of the firstborn son of a household. That inheritance was a double portion of the family's estate. The father allocated his estate to his sons, but the firstborn was given double what the others received.

In those days daughters were not given a part or share of the estate because they could marry outside of their family and their portion of the family's estate would become the property of the estate of the husband's clan carrying *another name* and this could not be allowed.

This was the case with the four daughters of Zelophehad in Numbers 27. They had no brothers and petitioned God through Moses to have the inheritance of their father deeded to them. Their request was granted with the condition that they marry within their clan.

Let us take a closer look at this story. In Numbers 27:3-7, the daughters of Zelophehad appealed to Moses to give them their father's inheritance. Their father had died in the wilderness and they did not have brothers. They said to Moses:

> *Our father died in the desert. He was not among Korah's followers, who banded together against the Lord, but he died for his own sin and left no sons.* **Why should our father's name disappear from his clan because he had no sons?** *Give us property among our father's relatives. So Moses brought their case to the Lord and the Lord said to him, "What Zelophehad's daughters are saying is right. You must certainly give them property as an inheritance among their father's relatives and turn their father's inheritance over to them."*

The Lord gave Moses further instructions regarding the transfer of an inheritance: where there were no sons, the inheritance was to be transferred to the daughters; where there were no daughters, the inheritance was to be transferred to the brother of the deceased; where there was no brother, then to the deceased's uncle; where there was no uncle, then to the nearest relative in his clan.

In Numbers 36:1-13, the clan of Manasseh realized that the daughters of Zelophehad could marry outside of their clan and as a result, their father's name would not live on and his allotted share of land would pass to another clan.

They also spoke to Moses:

> *When the Lord commanded my lord to give the land as an inheritance to the Israelites by lot, He ordered you to give the inheritance of our brother Zelophehad to his daughters. Now suppose they marry men from other Israelite tribes; then their inheritance will be taken from our ancestral inheritance and added to that of the tribe they marry into. And so part of the inheritance allotted to us will be taken away.*

In response to the Manasseh case, God said to Moses:

> *No inheritance in Israel is to pass from tribe to tribe, for every Israelite shall keep the tribal land inherited from his forefathers.*

Every daughter who inherits land in any Israelite tribe must marry someone in her father's tribal clan, so that every Israelite will possess the inheritance of his fathers.

From the dialogue above, it is clear that the transfer of property or tribal inheritance as it relates to birthright was and is a serious matter to God. What God instituted then was a foreshadowing of what was to come: Ephesians chapter 1, verses 14 and 18 make it clear that we are God's own possession and inheritance. He will not transfer us to another.

Esau Despised His Birthright

In Genesis 25:29-34, our reference Scripture, we see an interesting development with serious consequences. Esau, the son of Isaac, the son of Abraham, sold his birthright to his twin brother for a bowl of lentils. He treated his birthright lightly, not understanding that God Himself set up the birthright as a representation of His plan and purpose for a people to be manifested in the Christ. Christ as His firstborn secured an inheritance and the release of all spiritual blessings in heavenly places for all His sons. (See Ephesians 1:3.)

As a result of that one act, Esau not only lost his birthright—a double portion of the inheritance—but also the spiritual blessings that would have come down to him from his father. Instead of becoming the head of the family, he became his brother's servant. (See Genesis 27:39-40.) God responded to Esau's disregard in this way: *"'Was not Esau Jacob's brother?' the Lord says. 'Yet I have loved Jacob, but Esau I have hated, and I have turned his mountains into wasteland and left his inheritance to the desert jackals'"* (Mal. 1:2-3).

> *On Mount Zion will be deliverance; it will be holy, and the house of Jacob will possess its inheritance. The house of Jacob will be a fire and the house of Joseph a flame; the house of Esau will be stubble, and they will set it on fire and consume it. There will be no survivors from the house of Esau. The Lord has spoken* (Obadiah 1:17-18).

As a result of Esau losing his birthright and the spiritual blessings that should have been his, he became hostile toward his brother Jacob, and God had major issues with that. (See Obadiah 1:1-18 for

- *Our right* to live above sin and refuse to live below the standard of the life of Christ exemplified while on earth (see Heb. 9:26).
- *Our right* to live and have our being in the being of the Father.
- *Our right* to partake of the joy of eating from the mouth of the Father.
- *Our right* to become one with Father, Son, and Holy Spirit, by allowing Him to form Himself within our beings.
- *Our right* to live and walk daily in the joy and blessings of the Father.
- *Our right* to have the nations as our inheritance and the ends of the earth as our possession.
- *Our right* to walk in dominion, power, and authority.
- *Our right* to be Heaven's agreement on the earth, "*Your kingdom come, your will be done on earth as it is in heaven*" (see Matt. 6:10).
- *Our right* to be the will of the Father in the earth.
- *Our right* to be formed into the full measure of all the fullness of Christ.
- *Our right* to be His body in the earth, operating as priests and kings and giving Him a tabernacle to indwell so He can walk the earth.
- *Our right* to partake of His creative power and ability within us, which refuses to settle for anything less than God's best.
- *Our right* to embrace the revelation that "now are we the sons of God" (see 1 John 3:2 KJV), with His DNA flowing through our veins and a mandate to increase and bear much fruit and produce more sons.

Even more profound than these, God enforces His right to redeem us as His possession: "*Having believed, you were marked in him with a seal, the promised Holy Spirit, who is a deposit guaranteeing our inheritance until the redemption of those who are God's possession—to the praise of his glory*" (Eph. 1:13-14).

The purpose of exercising His rights is to reveal His intent as stated in Ephesians 3:10-12:

> *His intent was that now, through the church* (a community of nations, or an assembly or army of nations), *the manifold wisdom of God should be made known to the rulers and authorities in the heavenly realms, according to his eternal purpose which he accomplished in Christ Jesus our Lord. In him and through faith in him we may approach God with freedom and confidence.*

In other words, our embracing our birthright becomes a slap in the face of the enemy as we allow God to show Himself off in and through us.

Finally, when we consider our birthright, we must remember that:

- God *IS* and that He is a rewarder of those who *diligently seek Him* (see Heb. 11:6).

- Our born-again experience opens up the fullness of who God *is* and the richness of His estate for us. Not embracing and taking hold of His fullness equates to treating our birthright with disdain.

Let each of us, then, stop and ask the question: "What have I done with my birthright?"

ENDNOTES

1. Paul Keith Davis, *Thrones of Our Souls* (Florida, FL: Creation Press House, 2003).

2. Facts provide information regarding present circumstances or situations; however, facts are not necessarily truth, as the two are unrelated. Truth cannot be mistaken or shaken, for truth is Christ Himself. Truth then must always be our only reality and we must never mistakenly substitute facts for truth. We must be guided by truth always. "Let God be true and every man, situation, circumstance a liar."

Chapter 2

The Interpretation of the Promise and Covenant

*God promised a nation;
Abraham was looking for a son.*

For this reason Christ is the mediator of a new covenant, that those who are called may receive the promised eternal inheritance (Hebrews 9:15).

For most of us, our born-again experience came as a result of hearing a salvation sermon or someone's testimony. Salvation came at a very critical time in our lives, one where we may have been experiencing emptiness, depression, uncertainty, hopelessness, tragedy, or perhaps boredom.

The hope that came from hearing the salvation message opened our hearts to the Spirit of God and caused us to receive Christ as Lord and Savior. That same hope made us feel that Jesus would make everything right and our troubles would be over. It released the expectation that we were going to have a brand-new, trouble-free life that would manifest immediately.

Now, if we were being honest, we would admit that such a life really does not exist, and many of us ask *why*. What is really going on? This life should be better, but really it seems worse. Jesus Himself warned us that in this world we would have trouble. So instead of coming into the understanding of the *promise*, we pacify ourselves with countless sermons that cater to our circumstances and not to our birthright and the journey toward becoming *sons*.

God Promised a Nation; Abraham Was Looking for a Son

Many times we settle for a short-term solution rather than the long-term process of maturing as sons. This usually results in deferred hope, which indeed makes the heart sick.[1]

The *Word* of God has countless examples of short-term solutions for long-term manifestations. The story of Abraham and Isaac is a classic example of such.

Abraham was 75 years old when God called him and promised him that he would inherit the land of Canaan and give birth to a nation that would possess the land in the fullness of time. Eleven years later, Abraham had still not seen the manifestation of this promised son. He became concerned since he was indeed getting older. What he did not realize was that God was setting up a nation by means of a son and although a son could be manifested in nine months, nations would take time to come to full term. So, 25 years later, the son that would be instrumental in becoming a "community of nations" finally came forth. In Genesis 35:11, the Lord spoke to Isaac, this promised son, saying: *"I am God Almighty; be fruitful and increase in number. A nation and a community of nations will come from you, and kings will come from your body."*

In Genesis 28:3, Isaac, now an old man, blessed his second son, Jacob, with Esau's blessing, saying: *"And may God Almighty bless you and make you fruitful and add to you, and may you become an 'Assembly or army of Nations' "* (Literal Translation).

Abraham was looking for a son, but God's purpose was a nation.

Our Process Is the Same

Like Abraham's wait for Isaac, the process from our born-again experience to full sonship always seems to take a very long time. Quite often we become frustrated, and compromise steps in. This frustration comes as a result of seeking short-term solutions when God is seeking to establish something else in us—His image and likeness and His nature and character, which have eternal value and reveal us as His glory in the earth.

God's command to Abraham, Isaac, and Jacob was to be fruitful and increase in order to reproduce a *community of nations*. The command was the same that God gave to Adam in the Garden of Eden, and it remains the same today. God's agenda has always been to reproduce Himself in the earth, establishing communities and nations that have the mark of His image and likeness upon them and in the very fabric of their DNA.[2]

Unfortunately, the pressures around us seem to overpower and overshadow our true identity, calling, and purpose for living, and create a veil over the true interpretation of the promises of God. The one weapon we have in all of this as we continue on the journey and stay on the path is the covenant God has made with Abraham and fulfilled through the blood of Jesus. The price that was paid was too high to allow anything, whether heights or depths or demons or principalities, to distract us from the journey to full sonship.

How Can We Know That We Will Possess the Promise?

In Genesis 15:8, Abram asked God this question (after God promised that he and his descendants would inherit the land): *"O Sovereign Lord, how can I know that I will gain possession of it?"* God responded by making a covenant with Abram. (Note that Abram's name had not yet been changed to *Abraham*, which in Hebrew is translated as "father of a multitude.)

Verses 9-10, 12, 17-18 of Genesis 15 tell us God responded in this way:

"Bring me a heifer, a goat, a ram, each three years old, along with a dove and a young pigeon." Abram brought all of these to him, cut them in two and arranged the halves opposite each other; the birds, however, he did not cut in half. As the sun was setting, Abram fell into a deep sleep, and a thick and dreadful darkness came over him. When the sun had set and darkness had fallen, a

*smoking firepot with a blazing torch appeared and passed between the pieces. **On that day the Lord made a covenant with Abram** and said, "To your descendants I give this land, from the river of Egypt to the great river, the Euphrates."*

Now, to better understand what this means, let us examine Jeremiah 34:18. This is what the Lord says: *"The men who have violated my covenant and have not fulfilled the terms of the covenant they made before me, I will treat like the calf they cut in two and then walked between its pieces."*

One of the ways the Israelites made a covenant with each other was to cut an animal in half and walk between the pieces. By doing this they were saying that if either party did not honor its part of the agreement, what was done to the animal would be done to that party.

With that understanding, let's go back to our text in Genesis 15:17. After Abram cut the heifer, ram, and goat in two, he fell into a deep sleep and thick darkness covered him. (The heifer, ram, and goat were used as sin and guilt sacrifices).[3] In verse 17, a smoking firepot with a blazing torch passed between the pieces. The blazing torch was God Himself who passed through the pieces as He made His covenant with Abram *sure*. By so doing He made a bold statement: "If I do not keep My side of this covenant, let what happened to these animals, happen to Me." What is interesting to note is that God did not have Abram pass between the pieces; He actually made a one-sided covenant.

God did this because He was the only one to fulfill the promise made to Abram (see Heb. 6:13). Later in Chapter 17, God involved man when He confirmed His covenant and required Abraham (whose name was changed through this confirmed covenant) to circumcise every male who was with him. In verses 13-14, God tells Abraham: *"My covenant in your flesh is to be an everlasting covenant. Any uncircumcised male, who has not been circumcised in the flesh, will be cut off from his people; he has broken my covenant."*

The first covenant made with Abraham was a foreshadowing of the covenant made on the cross. Christ, in the form of man, took upon Himself the part of the covenant broken by Abraham's seed, and because Abraham himself did not pass through the pieces, Jesus had to become the sacrifice in order for full participation of the covenant to be made fully legal. Jesus passed through the pieces as His body was split apart on the cross and He bore the penalty of a broken covenant, ensuring and sealing the promise for all generations who would believe (see Heb. 9:15; 10:19-20).

Therefore, we have the full assurance that we will possess the promise of manifesting the fullness of our sonship, because Jesus Himself made it possible by His shed blood, broken body, and temporary separation[4] from His Father. The suffering, death, burial, and resurrection of Jesus Christ are the *fullness* of all we need to guarantee our success on the journey. We are now without excuse! Living a life below the full manifestation of "sons of God" is a sin which is missing the mark.

May the Spirit of God unfold this great revelation to your spirit, so that you will rise up and soar while on the journey.

ENDNOTES

1. Proverbs 13:12 states: *"Hope deferred makes the heart sick, but a longing fulfilled is a tree of life."* The word hope in the original language means expectation and it comes from the word gatekeeper. "Deferred" speaks of prolong, drawn-out, delayed. The word "make sick" speaks of to be worn, to be weak, sick, afflicted, grieved, infirmity, be wounded, woman in travail. Our hope in God and His promises is a present hope. Our lives are hid in God in Christ, which means our present position flows from a present and constant place of purpose in God. We are never operating in delayed, drawn out or prolonged purpose. God is here and now, and His purposes for our lives are here and now. Every day is a new adventure of fulfilling purpose, and bringing us closer to our formation into His image and likeness and Him finding Himself on the earth. Hope is deferred when our expectations are based on what, when, and how the Lord would fulfill His purposes in our lives, and when our expectations do not come to fruition, our hope dies and we die as well. But if our longing is to become the fullness of all that He is, then our gatekeeper stands with a face like flint and refuses to be diverted from the tree of life which is Christ, daily being nourished by His presence where our spirits remain strong, lively, merry,

and spring forth into new life looking forward with great anticipation for the fulfillment of His purposes each and every day. Romans 15:13 declares *"May the God of hope fill you with all joy and peace as you trust in Him, so that you may overflow with hope by the power of the Holy Spirit."*

2. Deoxyribonucleic Acid: the protein substance which controls the form and function of the cells and tissues of an individual. The composition of the genes of mankind. Genes determine heredity.

3. Leviticus 5:5-6, 17-18; Numbers19:1-10; Deuteronomy 21:1-9.

4. Jesus came from the Father and has always been in the presence of the Father. In John 14:10, He declares that He is in the Father Am and the Father in Him is (Literal Translation). The agony of Gethsemane was not primarily experiencing the fullness of the sufferings of the cross, but it was the pain of the separation of Jesus from the Father. Jesus did not die for sin, but He became sin. He was indeed a sin offering. The Father in His holiness cannot look upon sin, so for a brief moment separated Himself from His Son. That was the reason for Jesus' cry on the cross: "Father why hast Thou forsaken me." Words are inadequate to describe the effects of that separation. Years ago, in my quest to pursue God with every fiber of my being, I desperately asked the Lord to reveal to me my heart. In a moment, my world became pitch blackness of the worst kind; it felt like there was a great big chasm between God and me. Immediately, I knew I was experiencing the type of separation Jesus encountered on the Cross.

Chapter 3

The Lord Will Do Anything to Protect the Promise

Get rid of the slave woman and her son, for the slave woman's son will never share in the inheritance with the free woman's son. Therefore, brothers, we are not children of the slave woman, but of the free woman (Galatians 4:30-31).

THE PRICE TO PROTECT THE PROMISE

Throughout the journey, the Lord will do whatever He desires to ensure that you possess the promise of your sonship. Whatever He deems as a threat to the promise, He will remove! Key to this part of the journey is a surrendered heart, mind, soul, and body.

In John 17:26, Jesus prayed to the Father before leaving the earth: *"I have made you known to them, and will make it known that the love with which you loved me may be in them and I in them."* I am making reference to this verse at this point because I want us to pay close attention to the word *love*.

The word love in the Greek is *agape*[1], which means "unconditional or benevolent love." This benevolence, however, is not shown by doing what the person loved desires, but what the one who loves deems is needed by the one loved. In giving His Son, God gave not what man wanted, but what man needed as God perceived his need. It is God's willful direction toward man.

In turn, Jesus gives us a revelation of His Father's *agape* (unconditional love), which operates based on what He deems as our need and not based on our desires, to reveal that the Father derives great joy in loving us that way. He loves to display and express His *agape* in us. What gives the Father joy is to love us *in* His *agape* love.

The heart of the Father speaks: "My love for you is made known to you by not necessarily doing or satisfying what you think is best for you, but by doing what I know is best for you, and I take great pleasure in displaying such love, because it will bring out 'Me' from within you. It gives Me pleasure when I look at you and find Me."

God's Love Is Not Always Easy

Jesus embraced the cross because of the joy it gave Him to bring many sons to God. The method was not His first choice as a man, but the results far outweighed the method (see Heb. 12:1-3).

In Genesis 21:1-20, Abraham was asked to send his firstborn son Ishmael away from him and his people. This seems like a *very* harsh and heartless request. Why would God ask this? Whatever happened to the rights of the firstborn?

The "rights" of the firstborn son were secured by the law, but God's promise was sealed by a covenant.[2]

In this instance then, the rights of the firstborn were not legitimate as they related to possessing any rights to the promise because the promise was sealed by a covenant and not by law. The covenant promise outlawed the law, making ineffective the rights of the firstborn secured by the law. The firstborn's birthright was natural, whereas the covenant promise was supernatural. Supernatural is always superior to natural. The written code of the law is powerless when the covenant promise is at work or enforced. (Hallelujah!)

Ishmael (the firstborn) did not carry within his genes the fulfillment of the promise or the seed of the promise. God's love demanded that the firstborn be sent away in order to protect His greater purpose which would restore all of mankind to Himself, including the firstborn

Ishmael through covenant. What a price! Simply amazing! To one it is the perceived harshness of God and to the other it is God watching over His promise to fulfill it. In both cases it is the *agape* love of God in action whether through preservation, separation, or ultimately restoration.

We always focus on Abraham's test with Isaac, but the Word of the Lord says that Abraham was *"greatly distressed because of his son Ishmael."* Having to pack Hagar a bag of food and a skin of water was not an easy exercise in obedience for Abraham. However, obedience to God and stewardship of the promise took priority for him.

I am sure that there were lots of questions in Abraham's mind. Later, though, having successfully journeyed through the experience of giving up one son, Ishmael, and willingly paying the price of the grief it caused him to protect God's purpose in his son Isaac, Abraham was qualified for the next level of the ultimate sacrifice of the very promised son, the one in which the community of nations would come forth.

At that point, God was asking him to sacrifice the fulfillment of the actual promise he had waited 25 years to see manifested. This type of sacrifice equates to the death of a dream or the death of a vision, all for complete obedience to God to protect the promise. This experience proved to Abraham his total trust and confidence in God through the process of the journey. He had obeyed God for who He was as God and had not been sidetracked or controlled by temporary solutions or the resignation of thinking that he had advanced sufficiently in his pursuit of God.

The fact is that Abraham desired the fullness of God and not just a deposit of His presence. Unfortunately, we often stop at the deposit of the Holy Spirit within us and do not access the same Holy Spirit in His fullness to come into the fullness of the Father.

As a result of journeying at this level which was manifested in obedience, Abraham not only made room for himself and his immediate family to experience the fullness of the promise of God and of the blessings of God, but for entire generations then and now, to experience the same. Galatians 3:29, 3:14 declares that: "If we belong to Christ then we are Abraham's seed and heir to the promise, because the Father has redeemed us by the blood of Jesus Christ His Son in order that the blessings given to Abraham might come to us through Christ Jesus His Son, so that by faith we might receive the promise of the Spirit." (Author's paraphrase.)

We are under the blessing of that covenant. Jesus Christ made it possible by becoming the blood sacrifice and completing the other part of the contract in Genesis 15, as well as being Abraham's seed through the bloodline of Jesus, which began with Isaac.

Years later after Isaac's birth and the death of Sarah his mother, Abraham married Keturah in his old age and had other sons whom he also sent away. The Scripture states that he (Abraham) gave them gifts and sent them away from his son Isaac to a far land to protect the promise (see Gen. 25:5-6).

The *agape* love of God will remove anything within us and around us to establish the promise of the fullness of who He is in us as He journeys with us on the path (Way) to sonship.

Nothing is worth holding on to regardless of the price! Anything that jeopardizes the promise must be removed! Who knows how many generations to come would be affected by our decision to relinquish everything that would hinder the manifestation of the presence of God within us!

Endnotes

1. *Greek Lexical Dictionary*, from *The Hebrew Greek Key Study Bible, from King James Version* (Chattanooga, TN: AMG International Inc. D/B/A Publishers, 1991), #26.
2. Read Galatians chapters 3 and 4 for further clarification.

Chapter 4

No Covenant Without a Sacrifice, No Sacrifice Without an Altar

There he (Abraham) *built an altar to the Lord and called on the name of the Lord* (Genesis 12:8).

When an altar is built unto the Lord and a sacrifice made, God delivers our enemies into our hands.

The Oxford dictionary defines *covenant* as "a binding agreement (tight as compact powder) coming together, each grain in covenant with each other." *The Lexical Aid to the Old Testament* defines *covenant*[1] as "determination, stipulation, 'league and confederacy'; an ancient custom of ratifying solemn covenants by passing between the divided parts of victims." It was a treaty, alliance of friendship, a pledge, an obligation between a monarch and his subjects, a constitution. It was a contract accompanied by signs, sacrifices, and a solemn oath that sealed the relationship with promises of blessings for obedience and curses for disobedience.

The word *covenant* has its root in another word, *Barah*[2] and is defined as "in the sense of cutting like *Bara*"[3] and it means "to select; to feed; to render clear; choose; eat; manifest; give meat." *Bara* means "to create, form, make, produce, to cut, engrave, to carve. An activity that can be performed only by God." The word also means to "bring into existence," as used in Genesis 1:1.

A careful examination of the word *covenant* reveals the awesome integrity of God. It shows His unchangeable Word and ways as stated in Hebrews 6:13, 17-18,

> *"When God made his promise to Abraham, since there was no one greater for him to swear by, he swore by himself. Because God wanted to make the unchanging nature of his purpose very clear to the heirs of what was promised, he confirmed it with an oath. God did this so that, by two unchangeable things in which it is impossible for God to lie."*

God, as our only source and the source of all things, chose us in Christ Jesus before the foundation of the earth, set His seal of ownership upon us, and arranged it all in such a way that it cannot be changed. When God made the heavens and the earth, He was in covenant with what He made and that cannot be changed. (See Jeremiah 31:35-37.)

This is the depth of the covenant God has made with the heirs of salvation. The hope of this covenant is the reality of Jesus Christ in His heavenly ministry as High Priest (replacing the earthly high priest), entering the inner sanctuary behind the veil on our behalf, and granting us full access to our inheritance in the presence of the Father.

Jesus said in John 6:53, *"Unless you eat the flesh of the Son of Man and drink his blood, you have no life in you."* Jesus explained this statement at the Last Supper when He said, *"This is My body being given for you; do this in remembrance of me. This is the new covenant in My blood, being poured out for you"* (Luke 21:19-20 Literal Translation). In other words, unless we become true partakers of the body and blood of Jesus, we cannot be one with Him. His body and blood must replace our own; without that there is no life in us. Partaking of His body and blood translates to becoming one with Him in His suffering, death, and resurrection. We must eat *all* of the Lamb.

The taking of communion is the physical sign that reminds God of His covenant with Abraham's seed. It is an everlasting covenant. Yes! Every time we partake we are partaking of the wounds of His flesh and becoming one with Him, just as though we ourselves suffered those wounds. Circumcision of the heart takes place every time. God looks down and says "Yes" and through Christ in us we say "Amen."

The "Yes" and "Amen"

In 2 Corinthians 1:20, Paul declares, "In him [Christ] it has always been 'yes.' For no matter how many promises God has made, they are 'Yes' in Christ. And so through him the 'Amen' is spoken by us to the glory of God."

The word *yes*[4] speaks of "surely, truly, a strong affirmation, and doubtless."[5] The word *amen*[6] speaks of "truly—may it be so" and "surely—so be it."[7] This word comes from two other Hebrew words, *âman*[8], "to be firm, faithful, true," and *âmânâh*[9], which means "something fixed, covenant."

When we examine the words *yes* and *amen*, we notice the agreement between them. The word *promise* as used in 2 Corinthians 1:20 comes from the Greek word *epaggelia*[10], which means "to report or declare." It is primarily a legal term denoting "a summons or promise undertaking to do or give something." Used only with regard to the promises of God, the word speaks also of divine assurance. Therefore, when God makes a promise and then says *yes* to the promise and we say *amen* to the *yes*, a powerful marriage takes place that cannot be broken or separated by circumstances, trials, testing, hell, demons, angels, or any other such thing.[11]

Jesus Christ has already said "yes" to withhold no good thing from us. He has already said "yes" to the Father on our behalf. The Father awaits our *amen* (be it unto me according to Your "yes," Jesus) to release the promise as we journey on the path to our sonship.

All we need has already been provided. "Yes" from the lips of Jesus denies and defies the presence of any hindrances.

"Yes and Amen" Is God's Standard of Agreement

Often, we quote 2 Corinthians 1:29 with our own personal agenda in mind. God in His divine wisdom knows and understands our nature so well that He will not necessarily release the desires of our heart unless those desires become the desires of His heart for us. God is a jealous God, and He wants us all for Himself.

Every time, then, that God releases His hands to us, He does so to enable us to seek His face so that our *amen* will be to His glory. Our focus must be to give Him glory, to pay less attention to the thing or blessing and more attention to Him, His love, His faithfulness, His truth, all that He is. We must never shortchange God when it comes to revealing His glory in and through us. He is more interested in our relationship of intimacy with Him. The blessings automatically follow. As Jesus admonishes us, we must *"Seek ye first the kingdom of God, and his righteousness; and all these things shall be added unto you"* (Matthew 6:33 KJV).

God wants us to stretch ourselves in the secret place in Him. When we do so, we find all of His blessings and promises right there at our disposal. His desires become our desires, and He delights in granting them when asked. We have never been in lack; our only lack as believers is lack of intimacy with Him, which results in lack of revelation of who He is and what He has decreed concerning us.

God's Word is Himself. Only when we partake of Him by allowing His Word to consume us will He back up what He has spoken. As He draws nearer to us, our vision of Him becomes brighter and believing Him becomes so much easier. Taking hold of His promise, in turn, becomes easier, and we begin to be formed into His image and likeness. The excitement the Lord receives when He sees His image and likeness manifested in us causes Him to jump, spin, and dance with joy and shout to the Father, *"I praise you, Father, Lord of heaven and earth, because you have hidden these things from the wise and learned and revealed them to little children. Yes, Father, for this was your good pleasure"* (Luke 10:21).

No Sacrifice Without an Altar

We started this chapter talking about covenant and altars. There is no covenant without a sacrifice, and we understand now that the covenant was fulfilled with Christ as the sacrifice. The altar, however, is another thing.

No altar is ever built without the intention to sacrifice upon it. We see this in Scripture, particularly when Abraham, Isaac, and Jacob built altars unto God and offered sacrifices to Him in the form of slain animals.

On the journey and as part of our *amen* to God, He requires us to build an altar in our hearts and make a sacrifice of anything He desires on that altar. A sacrifice opens the heavens within us and above us and causes God to do what would otherwise not be done, to forgive what would otherwise not be forgiven, to release what would otherwise be held up and held back.

The power of the cross was not the cross but the sacrifice that hung there (Jesus Christ). Every time God made a covenant with man, He required a sacrifice. For every sacrifice there must be a place of offering (altar). The greatest place to offer up anything to God is from our hearts and the innermost secret parts of our beings, not just our lips. Our lips will then utter the fullness of the experience taking place within our beings.

Our place to offer up is from the hidden chambers within our souls, from the deepest part of our beings where only deep can call unto deep. Many times our sacrifices become lip service. We sing the songs and say all the right things, and yet we deny the power of God within our being. The altar must be built on the throne of our heart and every part of our being. It must be built upon our will, upon the thrones of our soul.[12] Our hearts, our entire being must become His throne![13]

An altar represents a place of meeting with God. Wherever an altar is built and a sacrifice is made, God shows up! Where the presence of God is, the presence of evil cannot remain. When an altar is built unto the Lord, God delivers our enemies into our hands.

We see this in Genesis 14:13-17, where we find Abram going to war, rescuing Lot, and defeating the enemies of Sodom. It's interesting to note that time was taken to mention that Abram was living near the great trees of Mamre. In Genesis 13:18, we see that *"Abram moved his tents and went to live near the great trees of Mamre at Hebron, where he built an altar to the Lord."* Watch this! Abram built an altar at Mamre. An altar ushers in the presence of the Lord. Abram dwelt at Mamre, and that meant he lived in the presence of the Lord. Abram didn't ask if he should go into battle—he didn't have to. The assurance of the presence of God was real to him because he had established an altar long before there was any threat of war. Abram won the battle before he ever fought it!

When an altar is built unto God within our beings, the enemy of our souls, manifested in the corrupt seed of the sinful nature within us and whose assignment is to kill, steal, and to destroy us, will have no power over us, our bodies, or our souls (emotion, will, intellect). The power of the sinful nature to exercise dominion over us will be extinguished and completely destroyed.

In Romans 2:29, Paul states,

> *"No, a man is a Jew if he is one inwardly, and circumcision is circumcision of the heart, by the Spirit and not by the written code. Such a man's praise is not from men, but from God."*

In other words, the everlasting covenant made in the flesh of man in Genesis 17 and fulfilled in the life of Christ Jesus produces (when acknowledged and accepted) true circumcision of the heart by the Spirit of God. Jesus fulfilled all righteousness so that we would be made the righteousness of God and remain in covenant with God. *"For them I sanctify myself, so that they too may be truly sanctified"* (John 17:19).

So, a permanent, acceptable sacrifice stands before God day and night that satisfies the Father and releases the fullness of the promise (our sonship), as *yes* in Christ and *amen* through Him by us for the glory of the Father. Hallelujah! Thank you, Jesus!

As we participate in this awesome experience of becoming a living sacrifice with an altar burning deep within our beings unto God, we can stand in full agreement with the Word of God and declare,

> *"No matter how many promises God has made, they are 'Yes' in Christ. And so through Him the 'Amen' is spoken by us to the glory of God. Now it is God who makes both us and you stand firm in Christ. He anointed us, set His seal of ownership on us, and put His Spirit in our hearts as a deposit guaranteeing what is to come"* (2 Corinthians 1:20-22).

I say *amen* to that!

ENDNOTES

1. *Lexical Aid to the Old Testament,* from *The Hebrew Greek Key Study Bible, from King James Version* (Chattanooga, TN: AMG International Inc. D/B/A Publishers, 1991), #1285.

2. *Hebrew and Chaldee Dictionary*, from *The Hebrew Greek Key Study Bible, from King James Version* (Chattanooga, TN: AMG International Inc. D/B/A Publishers, 1991), #1262.

3. Ibid., #1254.

4. *Greek Lexical Dictionary*, from *The Hebrew Greek Key Study Bible, from King James Version* (Chattanooga, TN: AMG International Inc. D/B/A Publishers, 1991), #3483.

5. Ibid., #3304.

6. *The Hebrew Greek Key Study Bible, from King James Version* (Chattanooga, TN: AMG International Inc. D/B/A Publishers, 1991), #543.

7. *Greek Lexical Dictionary*, from *The Hebrew Greek Key Study Bible, from King James Version* (Chattanooga, TN: AMG International Inc. D/B/A Publishers, 1991), #281.

8. *Lexical Aid to the Old Testament*, from *The Hebrew Greek Key Study Bible, from King James Version* (Chattanooga, TN: AMG International Inc. D/B/A Publishers, 1991), #539.

9. Ibid., #548.

10. *The Hebrew Greek Key Study Bible, from King James Version* (Chattanooga, TN: AMG International Inc. D/B/A Publishers, 1991), #1860.

11. Hebrews 9:16: "*In the case of a will it is necessary to prove the death of the one who made it, because a will is enforced only when somebody has died; it never takes effect while the one who made it is living. This is why even the first covenant was not put in effect without blood.*" The "will" of God has surely been enforced; the blood of Jesus sets the seal upon it. We can afford to say Amen.

12. Paul Keith Davis, *Thrones of Our Souls* (Florida, FL: Creation Press House, 2003).

13. In the book of Leviticus chapter 10:1-2, we see Nadab and Abihu, sons of Aaron and priests themselves, offering to God what God considered "strange fire." It was strange because it was not what God determines as worship or how

He accepts worship. We cannot bring artificial worship before the Lord. The fire that God accepts comes from burnt offerings which come from the best parts of the sacrifice as described in chapter 8:18-22. We cannot present to God our idea of worship. He has a prescribed way. We cannot fabricate our worship. It must come forth from the "fire" that comes from our sacrifices, when from our sacrifices God is given the best and the fattest part of our lives.

There were two ways to offer sacrifices as a form of worship to God. The external parts (the head, legs, etc.) were offered with incense added to it, but the inner parts and the fat were offered as "incense." God desires truth in our innermost parts. When He is allowed to establish truth within us, by removing the dross and forming Himself within, then what is released from our innermost being is considered incense to God. We become the incense; our lives become the sweet-smelling aroma going up to Him. Our external circumstances and situations must be brought before God in prayer and with worship as we lay them down before Him. Our worship then in the midst of the situations is considered a sacrifice of praise — the fruit of lips that confess His name (see Heb. 13:15).

SECTION II

The Deception of Mistaken Identity

"The God in Me Revealed."

Introduction

The Holy Spirit is the deposit we have been given guaranteeing our inheritance. What shall we do with Him, "the God within us"?

God is making sure that our hearts are pure enough to discern the deposit. The Holy Spirit was given to us on the day of our born-again experience. For some of us, it was on that same day that we were baptized with the Holy Spirit with the evidence of speaking in tongues. For others, it was later in our born-again experience. In either case, we often stop there, not discerning that the deposit of the Holy Spirit (which really is a gift from the Father) was to enable us and empower us to come into the fullness of the Godhead and to access the God within us (the Holy Spirit Himself)!

That deposit had far-reaching effects and eternal value and unlimited access to the person of Jesus Christ and our heavenly Father. Many of us have gone about our daily lives stuck at the point of our salvation experience. We have ignored (consciously or unconsciously) the presence of the Holy Spirit. (In Section II of the journey, we will examine "the God in me." We will learn where He is located and what hindrances there are to accessing Him.)

The main purpose of the deposit of the presence of the Holy Spirit within us is to reveal who Jesus is and by so doing, reveal who we are in Him.

Chapter 5

Who I Am... Is *in* the I Am!

Before I formed you in the womb I knew you, before you were born I set you apart, I appointed you as a prophet to the nations (Jeremiah 1:5).

In Jeremiah 1:5, God tells us, *"Before I formed you in the womb I knew you."* This is a familiar verse, but in order to fully grasp its meaning, we need to define some of the key words:

Before I formed you in the womb... The word *formed* in this verse speaks of "squeezing into shape, to mould into a form, to determine, fashion, purpose, to exist."[1] This definition sounds very much like that of the root word *Bara*, from which the word *covenant* came (as mentioned in Chapter 4).

I knew you... The word *knew* speaks of "to know, to ascertain by seeing, including observation, care, recognition, acknowledgement, acquaintance."[2]

Before you were born... Literal translation: "before you came out to go: bring forth, bring out."

I set you apart... The words *to set apart* speak of "to dedicate, prepare, purify, proclaim, sanctify."[3] We are purified and sanctified because the Lamb was slain before the foundation of the earth.

I appointed you a prophet to the nations. The word *appointed* speaks of "to visit (with friendly or hostile intent), to oversee, charge to inspect, review, to care for, look after, to be entrusted with."[4]

Now let us put this verse back together. Using our definitions, it reads:

> Before you took on manifest form or shape in the earth (of your mother's womb) I knew you. How is that possible? You were with me, in the spirit. You were one of the spirits that came forth from my breath and surrounds my throne, waiting to be assigned to the earth. Your first existence was not that first heartbeat in your mother's womb. I was acquainted with you and cared for you before the physical manifestation of your earthly existence.[5]
>
> You preexisted with me even as is clearly stated in Romans 8:29-30, *"Those God foreknew he also predestined to be conformed to the likeness of his Son, that he might be the firstborn among many brothers. And those he predestined he also called; those he called, he also justified (just as if you had never sinned), those he justified, he also glorified."*
>
> I also stated in Ephesians 1:4, *"He (God) chose us in him (Christ) before the creation of the world to be holy and blameless in his sight."*
>
> I stated again in Hebrews 12:9, *"How much more should we submit to the Father of our spirits and live!"*
>
> I determined before you came forth, before I said to you, "Go," that you were to be set apart for me (sanctified, purified, and dedicated to me).

God Said "Go!"

God is saying here that He took care of everything before you were manifested on the earth. He is making it clear that your path was predetermined. He made sure to first and foremost set you apart for Himself, because you came out of Him. Then, knowing the path you would have to walk, He purified you by applying the blood of Jesus to you, guaranteeing your redemption. How was that possible? As mentioned before, the Lamb was slain before the foundation of the earth. Mind-boggling, isn't it? This is the wisdom of the all-loving, all-knowing, all-seeing, gracious, and merciful God.

Let me explain further. Psalm 139:13-16 declares:

> *You have possessed my reins (inward parts). You wove me in my mother's womb. I will thank you for with fearful things I am wonderful (out of reverence for who you are, I am wonderful). Your works are marvelous and my soul knows it very well. My bones were not hidden from you when I was in secret. When I was woven in the depths of the earth, my embryo saw your eyes (your eyes saw my embryo); and on your book all my members of them were written; the days they were formed and not one among them or (not one was among them)* (Literal Translation).

Bible commentators have this to say concerning this verse: "Inward parts used of the seat of emotions and affection, the psychological aspect of man. The all-sovereign God is the Creator superintending both the psychological (inward parts) and physical (knit me) structure. In this as in all His works, He displays wonderful, i.e., supernatural powers. But the implication of the creative work is His intimate knowledge of His creation."

The Creator's work, however, covered not only the person concerned, *but also the experiences yet in store for that person.* Here again is the comfort implicit in the truth: the Creator plans all life; all our experiences are under sovereign control.

"The days that were formed for me." The Creator does not push out the boat of the individual's life to take its dance on the stream of time. The days were formed also. Even to this degree does He care for us.[6]

In other words, as spirit, God determined our path in life—whether it's perceived as good or bad—when we left His presence to take form in the earth. When He released the command "go," innate within the word was every experience we would ever encounter on our path back to Him. When conception takes place, God determines who He will release in that womb and what the experience of that one will be.

Job understood where he came from and declares it in chapter 10, verses 1-12. He brings the point home in verses 8-12:

Your hands shaped me and made me. Will you now turn and destroy me? Remember that you molded me like clay. Will you now turn me to dust again? Did you not pour me out like milk and curdle me like cheese, clothe me with skin and flesh and knit me together with bones and sinews? **You gave me life and showed me kindness, and in your providence watched over my spirit.**

In 1 Kings 22:19-22, we get a glimpse into this aspect of the spirit realm. The prophet Micaiah said:

I saw the Lord sitting on his throne with the host of heaven standing around him on his right and on his left. And the Lord said, "Who will entice Ahab into attacking Ramoth Gilead and going to his death there?" One suggested this, and another that. Finally **a spirit** *came forward, stood before the Lord and said, "I will entice him." "By what means?" the Lord asked. "I will go out and be a lying spirit in the mouths of all his prophets," he said. "You will succeed in enticing him," said the Lord. "Go and do it."*

The word used for *spirit* in this verse is *ruach*[7], which refers to the spirit and not the soul, *nephesh*.[8] When someone dies, the immortal *ruach* returns to God who gave it. The word means "air for breathing, the breath of one's mouth, i.e., the creative word of God." Genesis 2:7 speaks of the spirit of man as breathed by God into man.

Accepting this definition of the word *spirit*, we will now apply a similar scenario in the heavenly realm when God released the command for us to go, as translated in the original language in Jeremiah 1:5, *"Before you came out to go."*

God spoke in Heaven, saying:

> I need someone to go to the earth and to be Joe. Joe will pass through the birth canal of sin and be ravaged by the sin sickness of the world and become a victim of its schemes and devices, which *will* be manifested in many ways. The one aim of this sickness is to end in death and waylay Joe from fulfilling his assignment on the earth. All of this will take place before he finally comes to the narrow pathway I have reserved to meet with him. This

path leads to his identity, back to the Father. Who will *go* and become Joe?"

Right then, one of the little spirits that comes forth from the breath of God every time He exhales said, "Send me, send me, I will go." God then said, "Go."

As He said "Go," He applied the blood of the Lamb upon this little spirit, purifying him for the adventure he was about to have. The heavens resounded with the command and all of creation welcomed this addition to the earth that would be manifested one day as a son of God, to release the earth from its groaning (see Romans 8:18). This addition would cause all the enemies of Jesus to become the footstool for His feet.

Endnotes

1. *Lexical Aid to the Old Testament*, from *The Hebrew Greek Key Study Bible, from King James Version* (Chattanooga, TN: AMG International Inc. D/B/A Publishers, 1991), #3335/3334.

2. Ibid., #3045.

3. Ibid., #6942.

4. *Hebrew and Chaldee Dictionary*, from *The Hebrew Greek Key Study Bible, from King James Version* (Chattanooga, TN: AMG International Inc. D/B/A Publishers, 1991), #6485.

5. When God created man from the dust of the earth, what He released in that dust was His breath which was manifested as our spirit-man.

6. Donald Guthrie, et al, *New Bible Commentary*, 3d ed (Leicester, England: Inter-Varsity Press, 1970), 1208.

7. *Lexical Aid to the Old Testament*, from *The Hebrew Greek Key Study Bible, from King James Version* (Chattanooga, TN: AMG International Inc. D/B/A Publishers, 1991), #7307.

8. Ibid., #5315.

Chapter 6

The Assignment

We are therefore Christ's ambassadors, as though God were making His appeal through us (2 Corinthians 5:20).

When God said "Go" to *you*, He included both your assignment and your destiny in that directive. That assignment released you to the nations of the earth as God's mouthpiece or His spokesperson (ambassador). Paul makes this clear in 2 Corinthians 5:17-21 by making this statement:

Therefore, if anyone is in Christ he is a new creation; the old has gone and the new has come! All this is from God, who reconciles us to Himself through Christ and gave to us the ministry of reconciliation: that God was reconciling the world to Himself in Christ, not counting men's sins against them. And He has committed to us the message of reconciliation. **We are therefore Christ's ambassadors, as though God were making His appeal through us.** *We implore you on Christ's behalf: Be reconciled to God. God made Him who knew no sin to* **become** *sin for us, so that in Him we might become the righteousness of God.*

The voice of God continues to resound:

> I am sending you so that Heaven can have a representative on the earth, so that Heaven will always find *agreement* on the earth, when and where the will of Heaven is to be established on the earth. I send you with your assignment encoded within your spiritual DNA.

Our text confirms that God is saying He will cause us to be visited as a prophet to the nations. He will assign us to inspect, to care for, and look after the nations. God says:

> I will entrust you with the task and responsibility of enforcing My will, My Kingdom on the earth through lifestyle. My will be done on earth, as it is in Heaven. I am sending you to be My ambassador.

> Creation knows who you are and creation is eagerly waiting for you to come into the revelation of who you are and where you came from. (Now remember that both creation and created beings like the enemy know who you are.)

> When you "hit" the surface of the earth realm, through the birth canal of sin, your true identity in Me and the truth that you agreed to come to earth on this journey will be erased. As you are manifested on the earth, you will have the option to take several paths. But at the end of every path there is a narrow path (Way). There I will restore your identity in Me. Until such time you will unconsciously ask the question, 'Who am I?' and in so doing will attach yourself to anything or anyone that seems to give you a sense of identity and self-worth.

Moses Struggled With the Same Identity Issue

Moses is one of the greatest biblical examples of a man unaware of his identity. In Exodus 3:11, as God gave Moses his assignment to visit the nation of Egypt as a prophet (as God's mouthpiece) to release the Israelites from the bondage of slavery, Moses asked God an interesting question: *"Who am I that I should go to Pharaoh?"* Even more interesting is that in verse 13, God never responds to Moses' question, "Who am I?" Instead, God states who He, God, is: "I AM.... (I Am He who IS)".

Moses' identity was to be found in God Himself. When Moses discovered who God is—the God he had heard about, prayed to, talked about—that revelation totally transformed his life and thinking.

Now, we understand from Scripture that Moses would have had some initial awareness of the God of Abraham, Isaac, and Jacob, because Moses' father-in-law (Zipporah's father) was a priest and a descendant of Abraham's son Midian by his second wife, Keturah. Exodus 2:18 actually refers to Moses' father-in-law as Reuel, which means "friend of God"; and Exodus 3:1 refers to him as Jethro, which means "His excellence."

This priest of God would have taken Moses under his wings and taught him the ways of the God of Abraham, Isaac, and Jacob. Yet the revelation of God as *"I AM"* was not known to the Israelites or the Midianites.

When Moses asked, "Who am I?" God did not waste time explaining to Moses his (Moses') existence in Him; rather, He made a bold statement concerning Himself: "I AM"! In other words, God was saying to Moses, "If you (Moses) can grasp this revelation of Me, you have come to your narrow pathway, and you will know who you are or, better still, who 'I Am,' because 'I AM' sent you."

We have one main problem that faces us every day and its root is in our identity: We do not know who we are, and that is because we do not know who God is.

Who Am I? or Who I Am!

God is I AM! So, the question is not "Who am I?" but rather the statement "Who I am!" When we understand this, we can declare boldly, "Who I am... is *in* the I AM." Our identity is *in* the I AM. All that we are and ever will be is *in* the I AM who is within us! God in us!

Jesus understood that very well. He understood that He came from the Father and entered Mary's womb. He understood that He was on assignment. In John 14:10, He said: *"I am in the Father."* The literal translation expresses it this way: *"I in the Father am* (present tense), *and the Father in Me is* (present tense)." In other words, Jesus was saying, "I exist in the Father, because the Father is present in Me *in* Him. He is in me and I have My being in Him in Me." WOW!

The Holy Spirit has come to make His abode within us, so the Godhead is *in* us and we have our being in the Godhead in us. Therefore we must acknowledge the divine presence of God resident on the inside of us and understand the hindrances that prevent us from fully accessing the God within us.

Chapter 7

Hindrances to Accessing the God Within

If you hold to my teaching, you are really my disciples. Then you will know the truth, and the truth will set you free (John 8:31-32).

As mentioned before, mankind's primary problem is identity. The reason for this problem is the veil that was created between mankind's true identity relating to his origin with God and the distorted images that emerged when mankind came through the birth canal of sin, losing his true identity and purpose. That loss left a void and man has resorted to whatever is available to fill that void.

In this chapter we will examine some of the effects of these distorted images and how the veil (which Jesus has already destroyed) prevents the believer from accessing the very life of God resident within.

IDENTITY IS THE ROOT

The root cause of sin-sickness is a distorted identity. The problem began with mankind's identity being undermined, and this continues to be the problem. "If you eat the fruit, you will be like God," the serpent said to Adam and Eve. (See Genesis 3:5.) In truth, they were already like God.

Until we reach our narrow path (Way), we will always have an identity problem. No amount of binding and loosing will be able to cover it. Only an understanding of really "who we are" and "whose we are" can nip this thing in the bud and release us into the fullness of our assignment encoded in our commission to "go." Jesus gave His disciples—and by extension you and me—the same commission to "go."

Before we read any further in this chapter, let's do a little exercise by addressing the question I have asked many times as I was sharing with believers. When you look into the mirror, who do you see? Get a mirror, look at yourself, ask this question, and answer honestly.

Usually when I ask this question, I receive superficial answers. By that I mean answers that have to do with physical appearance and are mostly temporal, without eternal value. These are answers like the color of their eyes, what type of hair or skin they have. Often there are negative responses like too fat or too thin, ugly, abused, fearful, shy. Only on rare occasions will someone say "full of joy," "honest," a "hard worker," "committed," or identify himself or herself with his or her profession or family name.

The point is that however we see ourselves is, by extension, what we believe to be our identity. This, of course, is quite wrong! If we see ourselves as losers, mistakes, or unlovable, everything we do will be seen through those lenses. The same is true if we see ourselves through the labels of our positions, professions, or ministries.

Distorted Images versus Images of Truth

Let us for a moment examine the word *identity*. The word is defined as "personality, uniqueness, individuality (the thing that distinguishes me)."[1]

The word *personality* is a noun defined as being "a person, existence or identity or distinctive character." The word *unique* is an adjective defined as "being the only one of its kind, having no like or equal." The word *individual*, also an adjective, is defined as "having distinct character," but as a noun as "existence, character, especially when strongly marked."[2]

Wait a minute! Encoded in your identity is the truth that you are a person who exists with a distinctive character, a person who is one of a kind, having no like or equal. This means God created with great pleasure just one of you and the only one who has superiority over you is your Maker. You are also a person with distinct character, a character that is very strongly marked. You have been marked with the seal of the Holy Spirit of God, who indeed is your enabler, who empowers you to become the fullness of the very nature and character of God resident on the inside of you. A person generated by God with the DNA of God encoded within your spirit-man, identifying you as a *son* (no gender) of God and crying out, "Abba Father" as a witness within you. Now, this is truth! No fiction; no distortion.

Now, it is important to note at this point that images are formed by what we see. So if you keep looking into the mirror of distorted images[3] (those images that were formed through the very canal of sin that brought you forth into the earth realm), those images have now formed your history and shape your reality and identity.

In the Book of Psalms, King David testified to this when he said, *"In sin and iniquity I was formed in my mother's womb"* (see Psalm 51:5). Whatever you saw, whether by the spoken word or by behaviors directed at you, the root of it all is sin.

You might wonder how spoken words can be seen. Words are very powerful. In fact, God used words to create the earth and all that is in it. He makes it clear that life and death are in the power of the tongue. (See Proverbs 18:21.)

Words form pictures in our hearts, souls, and minds. When something contrary to truth is spoken to us, those words immediately form a picture. That picture creates a distorted image and leaves us paralyzed in our thinking concerning ourselves and our future. Soon we find ourselves vulnerable to the ravages of sin that seal the lie deep within the compartment of our souls. Every decision or choice we make is then tainted or colored by that distorted image always before us.

The Oxford dictionary defines the word *distort* as to "pull or twist out of shape, misrepresent or garble facts, motives and statements." So then, anything that misrepresents who God says you are, whether in thought, word, or deed, or anyone who misrepresents the very nature or character of God, creates a distorted image or view of you (or that person), your (or that person's) environment, and your (or that person's) relationships.

Images of Truth

Earlier, we connected with our origin and our true identity, which is in the I AM. Therefore, the mirror we will commit to look into from this point on is the image of truth, which is the Word of God. The Word of God is God Himself. Jesus is the Word made flesh.

The mirror of the Word of God is our only true point of reference in determining who we are. Now, we hear and read many Scriptures without the truth of the power of those Scriptures penetrating our being. We simply don't know our true history. The only history we know and understand is the one painted by the ravages of sin, and unfortunately, that has become our reality.

Praise the Lord, He has given to you and me access into the truth of our true origin, which empowers us to now embrace fully all that His Word imparts and releases us into true "sonship" and the very bosom of the Father. His Word becomes the narrow pathway that brings recall and reminds us that we were indeed with Him before the creation of the earth. We were with Him before the sperm and egg of our earthly parents came together to create a house for a little spirit birthed out of the breath of God. We were with Him before we came and took up residence on the earth in order to fulfill our higher call and purpose by ensuring that the Kingdom and will of Heaven is manifested on the earth, as God reconciles all things to Himself, whether thrones, or kingdoms, or created things. For all things were made for Him and by Him (see Colossians 1:15-20), so that the kingdoms of this world would indeed become the Kingdom of our God and of His Christ.

Examining the Truth of the Word

Many times I have read the following Scriptures to believers and could see in their faces that the words gave them hope for the moment. But when tested, they could not take hold of the reality of those Scriptures, including verses such as Genesis 1:26-28:

> *God said "Let us make man in our image, in our likeness."... So God created man in His own image, in the image of God He created him; male and female He created them. God blessed them and said to them, "Be fruitful and increase in number, fill the earth and*

subdue it. Rule over the fish of the sea and the birds of the air and every living creature that moves on the ground."

That command was not just for Adam. God also gave it to Abraham, Isaac, Jacob, and to you and me. That's the truth!

Colossians 1:22 says, *"But now He* [God] *has reconciled you to Christ's physical body through death to present you holy in His sight without blemish and free from accusation."* That's truth!

Jude 1:2 tells us, *"To Him who is able to keep you from falling and to present you before His glorious presence without fault and with great joy."* That's truth!

Isaiah 62:5 tells us, *"As a bridegroom rejoices over his bride, so will God rejoice over you."* Hallelujah. That's truth!

In light of all we spoke about in this chapter, you should now be able to examine the Word of God with a new level of understanding. In doing that, you will be better able to embrace fully all that He says as the fullness of what He has ordained for you while you complete your assignment in the earth realm.

Go forth and partake of the Word and be filled! Be empowered to become the fullness of all Jesus Christ died for, in fulfilling the covenant the Father made with you to restore you fully to the place you had with Him before the world began.

Endnotes

1. *New Lexicon Webster's Dictionary* (New York, NY: Lexicon Publication Inc., 1987).

2. Ibid.

3. Some examples of distorted images: low self-esteem—inferiority complex created by the spoken word. Intimidation, fear in its various forms: people, failure, the dark, the future. (Fear creates limitations.) Abuse in its various forms: physical, mental, verbal, emotional, and sexual. Manipulation—better known as control and in biblical terms witchcraft—operates in various forms and environments. Untruth—being true to form but not operating in truth. Self-exaltation: superiority

complex which really is an inferiority complex. Pride in its various forms: false humility, comparison, competition. Poverty: spiritually, emotionally, psychologically, materially. Common symptoms: feelings of hurt, shame, rejection, abuse, abandonment, unforgiveness, anger, woundedness.

Chapter 8

The Battle Begins—Part I

The woman saw that the fruit of the tree was good for food and pleasing to the eye, also desirable for gaining wisdom (Genesis 3:69).

We have now come to understand the truth concerning our true identity and inheritance in God. We are not merely on a religious quest, but rather we are awesome representations of our Father and God in the earth realm. We understand also that we existed back before the creation of the world. We were not a mistake or even a well-planned thought by our parents. No! God in His sovereign wisdom kept us hidden in Him until He decided to make us known to the earth realm.

I have a little statement I normally have my audiences repeat whenever I am presenting this subject. It goes like this: "I am a living, speaking spirit, birthed out of the heart, mind, and mouth of God, with the ability to create even as God did."

We must now understand our makeup. As a spirit being we cannot operate legally in the earth realm without a body. As stated in Genesis 2:7, *"The Lord God formed man from the dust of the ground and breathed into his nostrils the breath of life, and man became a living being"* (AMP).

The wombs of our mothers were the incubator that formed our bodies, giving us legal access to operate on the earth. God's breath released us as the spirit that came from Him into that body.

The perfect example of this is the Christ (spirit). He came forth into the earth realm having had His earth suit incubated in the womb of Mary to be manifested as Jesus Christ in order to have legal access in the earth as the last Adam.

The composition of a living being is one that comprises a spirit, soul, and body. In Hebrews these two words *ruach* and *nepehesh* are used to describe the full makeup of a living being.[1] Many times Scriptures are quoted describing man as a human being. The use of this term is an inaccurate translation of the intended word, which should have been translated as "living being," because a human being is defined as one with a body and soul. God sent us forth in the earth with a triune makeup.

Our spirits enable us to be fully connected to Him as our only source and Father. Our souls enable us to relate to our environment, and our bodies give both spirit and soul a house from which to operate legally. If we were just floating about as spirits only, we would be ineffective on the earth. That is why demonic spirits are always on the lookout for an open door into an individual whereby they are able to make a home for themselves. Outside of sin, demons would have absolutely no legal right to possess the bodies of mankind. God created our bodies for His habitation and His alone.

We will now examine how man moved from connecting to God, spirit to spirit (man's spirit dominating and influencing his environment through the soulish part of himself—his emotions, intellect, and will), to having the roles reversed, to man being dominated by his body and soul, with hardly any real dominance coming forth from his spirit. Mankind is classified as three-dimensional (body, soul, and spirit), rather than triune (spirit, soul, and body) just as the Godhead is triune—Father, Son, and Holy Spirit.

Let us examine how the reversal of these roles has affected us on a daily basis and as a result hindered us from coming into the fullness of our inheritance. We will do this by taking an in-depth look at mankind before and after the Fall.

Mankind Before the Fall

In Genesis 2:1-25, we see that man was created in the image and likeness of God. He was sinless and naked, feeling no shame because he was clothed in the glory of God. He was in full communion with God, and the life and fullness of God was manifested in him. Man walked in full authority and power to rule and reign on earth. (This is what I call the *dominion mandate*.) Man had full ability to make godly choices. He was governed by his spirit, not by his emotions, intellect, and senses (which make up the soulish realm). Nor was he ruled by his physical body.

Man ate daily from the tree of life, which guaranteed eternal life. Man was not created to die; death was never on God's agenda. God was very pleased with the body He created out of the dust. He said it was very good.

The Tree of Life

Genesis 2:9 states,

The Lord God made all kinds of trees grow out of the ground; trees that were pleasing to the eye and good for food. In the middle of the garden were the tree of life and the tree of the knowledge of good and evil.

The word *life*, when speaking of the tree of life (*chay*) is defined in Hebrew as "alive, fresh, strong, quick, running, springing, lifetime, lively." It comes from the root word *Châyâh*, which means "to live, to be whole, to be kept alive, nourishing, to preserve, to quicken, to promise life, to restore to life." These definitions make it clear that God's intention was that He (God) would have a body on the earth to walk in and operate through for all eternity. As long as man kept eating from the tree of life, man would never die and man would reproduce life in his offspring. God would have many images of Himself in the earth, uninterrupted by death.

Mankind After the Fall

In Genesis 3:1-24, we see mankind in a different light. Man's disobedience results in separation from God and the tree of life. For the first time, man is no longer covered with the glory of God, but has now made girdles[2] from fig leaves[3] as he attempts to hide his shame and disappointment. It is very important to note at this point that sin stripped man of his covering of God's glory and exposed him to defilement and dishonor. When man sinned, not only did he dishonor himself, but he dishonored God as well—until then, man had been the glory of God in the earth.

God in His loving-kindness saw to it that the enemy was not going to succeed in diverting His purpose by dishonoring His image in the earth, so He removed the fig leaves and replaced them with a covering (animal skin) made from a blood sacrifice. This sacrifice (the shedding of the blood of an animal) pointed to the day when the last Adam (Christ) would restore man to his former position of honor through the purity of His sacrificial blood. Man's restoration encompasses the glory of the Lord as his garment or covering once again. Our greatest cry in this hour is to see the glory of the Lord face-to-face, and Christ has fulfilled that. The glory of God is about to rise up within a people in this hour who will be true carriers of the glory of the Father, Son, and Holy Spirit and the very fragrance and atmosphere of Heaven. That is the inheritance of all those who diligently seek Him, embracing and partaking of the richness of this truth.

After the Fall, man inherited the "sinful nature." Satan was no longer on the *outside* of man, but his seed (the sinful nature) now resided in man. The sinful nature now impersonated the true personality of man and as a result caused man to live below the standard for which he was created. (See Roman 7:14-25.) A veil was now present, separating the spirit of man from his soul and body. (See 2 Corinthians 4:4 and Hebrews 10:19-22.) Man became self-conscious instead of God-conscious; self-governed instead of spirit-governed. Man had eaten from the tree of the knowledge of good and evil. Why was that so bad?

The Tree of the Knowledge of Good and Evil

Genesis 2:17 states, "*You must not eat from the tree of the knowledge of good and evil, for when you eat it you shall surely die.*" Genesis 3:6 also says, "*When the woman saw that the fruit of the tree was good for food and pleasing to the eye, also desirable for gaining wisdom, she took some and ate it.*"

The Battle Begins—Part 1

The Hebrew word for *knowledge* has both a positive and negative interpretation. In Hebrew, the word means "knowledge gained through the senses (the soulish area: feelings, eyes, ears, taste, touch, intellect, will)." Man was created to be governed by his spirit, influenced only by God, who is all-knowing, all-seeing, all-powerful. Man did not need to look to his environment or circumstances (seen through the lenses of his senses), to communicate to him in order to gain knowledge. That same Hebrew word for *knowledge* speaks of insight, intelligence, understanding, wisdom, and cunning.

The positive definition of the word speaks of wisdom, which is defined as enlightenment and discernment, and understanding, which is defined as recognition and comprehension, intelligence and insight. Yet when this kind of knowledge is acquired through the senses, it creates death.

The power of knowledge gained only through the senses creates a self-idolatry of man's own fallen nature and releases the very spirit of lucifer when he sought to exalt himself above the throne of God, believing that he no longer needed God and forgetting that he was just a created cherub. I call this behavior "having a touch of mistaken identity." Lucifer did this because his beauty and access to the very presence of God went straight to his head, which caused his position to be taken from him, and he was thrown to the earth to be made a footstool.

Ezekiel 28:12-15, 17 gives us some insight into this. Speaking of lucifer, whose name was changed to satan, meaning the "accuser of the brethren" or "deceiver," it states:

> *You were the model of perfection full of wisdom and perfect in beauty. You were in Eden, the garden of God; every precious stone adorned you: ruby, topaz and emerald, chrysolite, onyx and jasper, sapphire, turquoise and beryl. Your settings and mountings were made of gold; on the day you were created they were prepared. You were anointed as a guardian cherub, for so I ordained you. You were on the holy mount of God; you walked among the fiery stones. You were blameless in your ways from the day you were created till wickedness was found in you.* **Your heart became proud on account of your beauty, and you corrupted your wisdom because of your splendor. So I threw you to the earth; I made a spectacle of you before kings.**

What a powerful revelation of corrupted power and wisdom. The tree of the knowledge of good and evil was indeed a true representation of satan himself. Partaking of its fruit produced his nature and character in man and continues to reproduce that nature. The result of that nature is death!

The negative definition of the Hebrew word for *knowledge* confirms this. It speaks of cunning, which is defined as slyness, craftiness, caginess, subtlety, slipperiness, trickery, imposture, deceit, hypocrisy, falsehood, cleverness, artfulness, intelligence, imagination, resourcefulness, guile, and untruthfulness. *Intelligence* is defined as "rational, logic, reasoning mind."[4] Clearly, one can see that knowledge acquired through man's senses will produce death. What appears to be good will eventually turn to evil. Adolph Hitler is a typical example of such. The good he started with had evil intent. The good made him a self-idolater of his good works.

Now let us examine further the words *good* and *evil* in context to the tree of knowledge.

The word *good* in this Scripture (*tov*) is defined in Hebrew as "pleasant, delightful, precious, correct, practical, moral goodness, beautiful, convenient, sound, righteous, economic benefits, excellent, joyful, cheerful, virtue, wisdom, lively, fruitful, kind, happiness."[5]

The word *evil* (*ra*) is defined as "inferior quality, wicked, noxious (unhygienic, poisonous), mischievous, injurious, unpleasant, hideous, malignant, hurtful, fierce, giving pain or causing unhappiness, bad, wild, moral deficiency, misfortune, adversity, a bad thing which someone does, a calamity which happens, death, the inability to come up to good standards."[6]

Therefore, partaking of the tree of the knowledge of good and evil will cause us to believe that we are good people because we are doing good things, yet the sinful nature lurks in the background with its hidden agenda, waiting for the opportune time to strike. Once it does, it can produce death through the evil the same tree can and has produced in all of mankind.

We have often believed that the forbidden fruit was an apple. The truth of God now reveals the true nature of the fruit. The fruit of the tree of life was indeed partaking of all of the fullness of God, with a promise of eternal life as man governed the earth in full dominion,

The Battle Begins—Part 1

power, and authority, being controlled by the presence of the God within him.

The fruit of the tree of the knowledge of good and evil was the very nature of satan, producing in man self-idolatry and self-righteousness, removing his total dependence on God, acting in the same rebellion satan operated in as he corrupted the wisdom of God as his own by trusting in his own ability to overthrow God from His throne. This fruit will always produce death and all those who partake of it die a spiritual death. This is the sin that ravages mankind as he comes through the birth canal of sin. This fruit has indeed produced sin and sin results in death. First Corinthians 15:56 tells us that the sting of sin is death, and Romans 6:23 says the wages of sin is death.

The word *fruit* from the Hebrew *periy* is translated as "fruitful, reward," and comes from the root word *parah*, translated "to bear fruit, to increase, to grow, to bring forth."[7] Therefore, eating from either tree will reproduce and increase after its own kind. The fruit of life is life, which is Christ. Life will reproduce life. The reward for life is life. Likewise, the fruit of death is death. Death will reproduce death. The reward of death is death. Both will increase, grow, and bring forth after its own kind. This is the principle of nature. We must say *no* to the propagation of the seed of satan!

God's intent as mentioned before is to confound the powers that be by showing us forth in all His fullness, in the glory that lucifer once had. That glory and access to the presence of God belongs to us. It is our inheritance. God had never replaced lucifer's position until now, through the Church.[8] (See Ephesians 3:10-11.) Taking hold of the understanding of what God is releasing to His people in this hour is pertinent to the unfolding of the fullness of the truth of God being revealed in our own lives.

As you continue on the journey, keep your heart and spirit open to drink of the richness of this God that you have heard so much about, and long to come into a greater understanding of His purpose for your life.

Endnotes

1. *Lexical Aid to The New Testament* – #5315 – soul, spirit, mind, a living being, life. #7307-Spirit, breath. When relating to man,

ruach (7307) and *nephesh* (5315) must be combined. Man is a living being which comprises a spirit, soul, and body. When relating to the Holy Spirit, (*ruach*) only is used. The spirit does not have the composites of soul and body. The Christ man Jesus took up the form while on earth to be able to identify with man.

2. The word *girdles* in Hebrew is defined as "a belt for the waist," from the root word *chagar*, which speaks of "to be afraid, restrain on every side." Prior to the Fall man was unacquainted with fear, but now he says, "*I heard your sound in the garden, and I was afraid, for I am naked (uncovered) and I hid myself*" (Gen. 3:10).

3. Fig leaves in the Hebrew & Chaldee Dictionary speak of "lamentation, heaviness, and mourning" and come from the word *groan*. (#8386, 578). The fig leaves represent the groaning and heaviness of man's own effort.

4. *New Lexicon Webster's Dictionary* (New York, NY: Lexicon Publication Inc., 1987).

5. *Lexical Aid to The Old Testament,* from *The Hebrew Greek Key Study Bible, from King James Version* (Chattanooga, TN: AMG International Inc. D/B/A Publishers, 1991), #2896.

6. Ibid., #7451.

7. *Hebrew and Chaldee Dictionary,* from *The Hebrew Greek Key Study Bible, from King James Version* (Chattanooga, TN: AMG International Inc. D/B/A Publishers, 1991), #6529 - #6509.

8. The Church here refers to the true Church of Jesus Christ, the organism and not an organization. An organization must be maintained and supported by those who built it. An organism is a living being or entity adapted for living by means of organs separated in functions but dependent on one another.

Chapter 9

The Battle Begins—Part 2
The Victory Won

When He had received the drink, Jesus said, "It is finished." With that he bowed his head and gave up his spirit (John 19:30).

AT THE CROSS

Our restoration was taken care of in full on the cross. In Mark 15:37-39 we read, *"With a loud cry, Jesus breathed his last. The curtain of the temple was torn in two from top to bottom. And when the centurion, who stood there in front of Jesus, heard his cry and saw how he died, he said, 'Surely this man was the Son of God.'"*

Hebrews 10:19-23 reads:

> *Therefore, brothers, since we have confidence to enter the Most Holy Place by the blood of Jesus, **by a new and living way opened for us through the curtain, that is, His body,** and since we have a great priest over the house of God, let us draw near to God with a sincere heart in full assurance of faith, having our hearts sprinkled to cleanse us from a guilty conscience and having our bodies washed with pure water. Let us hold unswervingly to the hope we profess, for he who promised is faithful.*

At the cross, we see mankind restored as Jesus more than pays the price for the Fall and fulfills the covenant God made with Abraham. We see the veil that came in the form of the sinful nature—which caused the separation of man from his spirit man and having full access to the Father of his spirit (see Heb. 12:9b)—being ripped apart and completely destroyed, once again giving man full access into the presence of the Father. We see man being restored to his place of full power and dominion and the honor he enjoyed before creation and in The Garden in the presence of the Godhead, where his spirit ruled. We see man having the power to exercise complete power over the very nature of satan (the sinful nature) as Jesus destroyed the sinful nature through His own body, by becoming sin itself for a moment. We see the image and glory of God being restored to man once again.

In Romans 5:8, we see the magnitude of the power of the cross and the blood that flowed from it. It states, "*God demonstrates his own love for us in this: While we were still sinners* [yet caught in the lie of the deception of the tree of the knowledge of good and evil] *Christ died for us.*" Romans 5:10-11 states, "*If, when we were God's enemies we were reconciled to him through the death of his Son, how much more, having been reconciled, shall we be saved through his life!* [as we partake of the tree of life once again]. *Not only is this so, but we also rejoice in God through our Lord Jesus Christ, through whom we have now received reconciliation* [back to man's original status as a son of God]."

Chapter 10

The Battle Rages—Part I

For I have the desire to do what is good, but I cannot carry it out (Romans 7:18).

To understand how the battle rages, we now address each area of our triune being, bearing in mind that Jesus paid the ultimate price to ensure that we win the battle that continues to rage between the sinful nature and the spirit of man. Remember also that God the Father held nothing back to ensure the fulfillment of the promise so that we may partake of the fullness and richness of our inheritance in Him and in His inheritance in us. Jesus was manifested to destroy the works of the enemy, and greater is He that is in us (the Spirit of God) than he that is in the world (see 1 John 4:4).

It is important to reiterate once again that hindrances to accessing the life of God within create a shadow over our true identity. Let us now examine spirit, soul, and body. Who rules daily?

THE FIGHT FOR RULERSHIP

In Romans 7:15-20, Paul says:

> *I do not understand what I do. For what I want to do I do not do, but what I hate I do. And if I do what I do not want to do, I agree that the law is good. As it is, it is no longer I myself who do it, **but it is sin living in me. I know that nothing good lives in me, that is, in my sinful nature.** For I have the desire to do what is good, **but I cannot carry it out.** For what I do is not the good I want to do; no, **the evil I do not want to do—this I keep on doing.** Now if I do what I do not want to do, **it is no longer I who do it, but it is sin living in me that does it.***

Paul recognized that he was a spirit being with a soul that operated in a body. He understood at this point the behavior of spirit, since he had identified that God is the Father of spirits and certain behavioral patterns are not of the nature and character of his Father. That meant there had to be yet another entity operating on the inside of him at the same time. He was aware of a battle raging on the inside.

The revelation of this diabolical situation is the first step to Paul's deliverance from this exposed entity (the sinful nature), and the appropriation of the fullness of the price Jesus paid for him on the cross, when He destroyed this entity once and for all, making an open spectacle of it. Paul, having appropriated what Jesus did, must now walk in full victory over this entity, regaining power and dominion over it.

He confirms this great revelation by sharing the following with us in Romans 8:3-4:

> *What the law was powerless to do in that it was weakened by the sinful nature, God did by sending His own Son in the **likeness of sinful man to be a sin offering. And so he condemned sin in sinful man,** in order that the righteous requirements of the law might be fully met in us, who do not live according to the sinful nature but according to the Spirit.*

Paul is well on his way to operating in the fullness of his inheritance as a son of God. Thank God for revealing the mysteries that have been hidden and sharing with us the bounty of His love, His grace, His mercy, and His restorative power. Hallelujah!

You might ask at this point, exactly how does this force—the sinful nature—operate? Paul goes on to explain in verses 5-8:

Those who live according to the sinful nature have their minds set on what that nature desires; but those who live in accordance to the Spirit have their minds set on what the Spirit desires. The mind of the sinful man is death [that mind operates from the sap that flows from the tree of the knowledge of good and evil], *but the mind controlled by the Spirit is life and peace* [that mind is the mind of Christ. The mind of Christ operates from the very life that flows from the heart of the Father]. *The sinful mind is hostile to God. It does not submit to God's law,* **nor can it do so. Those controlled by the sinful nature cannot please God.**

First Thessalonians 5:23 states, "*May the very God of peace, sanctify you wholly and I pray that God, that your whole spirit and soul and body (notice the order) be preserved, blameless unto the coming of our Lord*" (Literal Translation).

Now the spirit is that part of our triune being that is fully God-conscious and communes with God. Our soul is that part of our triune being that relates to our environment and enables our spirit to express its thoughts. This area is conscious of both self and environment. Our body is the house from which our spirit and soul operate. It is the place of residence for the habitation of the Lord. Paul describes it as the temple of God, the place at our point of salvation where the Holy Spirit takes up residence. The body as it relates to the Hebrew meaning for *temple* is translated as the Holy of Holies of the presence of God.

The following Scripture verses will bring us to a level of understanding regarding God's purpose for the body.

Ephesians 3:19 says, "*To know this love that surpasses knowledge—that you may be filled to the measure of all the fullness of God.*"

First Corinthians 3:16: "*Know ye not that your body is the temple* [Holy of Holies] *of God and that the Spirit of God dwells* [makes his abode, habitation] *in you.*"

First Corinthians 6:19 KJV tells us, "*What? know ye not that your body is the temple* [Holy of Holies] *of the Holy Ghost which is in you, which ye have of God and ye are not your own?*"

Second Corinthians 6:16 KJV says, "*What agreement has the temple of God with idols? For you are the temple of the living God, as God has said: "I will dwell in them, and walk in them; I will be their God, and they shall be My people."*

Colossians 2:9-10 says, *"All the fullness of the Deity* [Father, Son, Holy Spirit] *lives in bodily form, and you have been given fullness in Christ."*

For most of us, conceptualizing our bodies as a habitation for the Holy Spirit is very difficult. We say it, but there is no connection between what we say and the reality of it. The reason for this is that we cannot fathom where the Holy Spirit finds rest within us. If we agree that we have a spirit that dwells within us and the image in the mirror is not the full reality of who we are, if we understand that the spirit man who dwells within us gives us our true identity, then wherever our spirit man dwells, the Holy Spirit also dwells.

The diagram in Chapter 12 gives us a glimpse of the spirit part of us that is resident within. We see how the battle rages on a daily basis with our enemy using deception to keep the veil (the sinful nature) over our soul and spirit—even though Jesus has already rent the veil and utterly destroyed it. This deception hinders us from accessing the fullness of the presence of the Holy Spirit at a level of communion that, if we were aware, would do anything to ensure and maintain our freedom from its bondage.

Let me explain further. When we receive Jesus as Lord, the Spirit of the Lord immediately comes and makes His abode within our regenerated spirit man. The primary reason for this is to restore our spirit man back to the Father and allow the Father through His Spirit to once again have His abode within us. The secondary reason is to enable our spirit man to grow and become strong so it can operate in the dominion power it was given in the beginning, rising up against the forces of darkness that have controlled the atmosphere of our souls from the time we came forth from the birth canal of sin. Our spirit man is immediately renewed and restored, but our soul with all its idols, thrones, and history must be cleansed.

The main enemy of the soul is not satan, but the seed of satan, which is the sinful nature man inherited after the Fall. Before the Fall, man had a spirit, soul, and body. There was no mention of a fourth entity called the sinful nature. Man's disobedience in partaking of the fruit of the tree of the knowledge of good and evil released the very nature and character of satan—the sinful nature—in man. So instead of man just being triune in nature, a fourth nature invaded the very soul of man, which represents the area of his senses, will, emotions, intellect, and mind.

"When the woman saw that the fruit of the tree was good for food and pleasing to the eye, and also desirable for gaining wisdom, she took some and ate it" (Gen. 3:6). The decision to eat was made from the area of the soul and not the spirit man. So the enemy has influenced, manipulated, and dictated to this area of man from the time of the Fall until now. Mankind believes that they make their own decisions, but unless the spirit man rules because God rules, then all other decision-making is directed and controlled by the sinful nature resident within the soul of man.

The sad thing about this is that most believers are convinced that their enemy is external. Satan has capitalized on that deception for a long time, keeping believers in a place of defeat and discouragement. They feel the need to go forward but are unable to break the chains that have bound them because they are unaware of the fourth nature within them. Believers spend much time binding and loosing the devil, and yet the victory seems to be eluding them. God never intended for us to be governed by external circumstances. He empowered us to enable us to be governed from within by His Spirit, releasing our spirit man to operate in dominion power—the power that governs the area of our soul where the sinful nature took up residence and, by extension, the situations and circumstances that arise around us on a daily basis.

Our reaction or response to an external situation is a clear indication of the atmosphere within us. One of the ways the sinful nature has been able to succeed in hiding itself within our souls is to impersonate itself into our very personalities. I mentioned that earlier when we dealt with the effects of the Fall. That nature came along with us as we passed through the birth canal of sin. That nature knows our history and also knows what makes us "tick." It manipulates us and dictates to our souls what pattern of behavior we will follow.

Remember—the biggest deception of the fruit of the tree of the knowledge of good and evil is that the knowledge was gained through the senses, and with that knowledge evil is hidden within the good the tree produces.

Most believers make decisions or judgments based on their senses: what it looks like, sounds like, and—the most common one of all—what it feels like. The sinful nature uses history to keep believers tied to the events of the past. This determines their identity, their reality, and their ability or inability to cooperate with God in becoming the fullness of all that Christ died for. Pain, disappointment, hopelessness, discouragement, depression, lost dreams, fear, and all the other maladies exist within the soulish area of believers, rooted in the sinful nature, shaping and impersonating their personalities. That is why Paul had such a difficult time with the sinful nature and said, *"What I want to do, I do not do, but what I do not want to do I do."* If we are honest, this very often is the cry of our hearts as well.

Chapter 11

The Battle Rages—Part 2
Our Triune Being

Those who live according to the sinful nature have their minds set on what that nature desires; but those who live in accordance with the Spirit have their minds set on what the Spirit desires (Romans 8:5).

Time must be taken to address this area of our triune being and to ensure that we do whatever is necessary to embrace the power of the Spirit of God within to enable us, so that we can look this sinful nature "eyeball to eyeball," refusing to submit to its ways and schemes. This nature has one assignment—to destroy us by causing satan to multiply his seed in the earth through us, if that were possible.[1]

Now we must understand that within the soul there are many compartments, some the Holy Spirit will reveal to us and others He alone has access to. Through the experiences we have encountered over the years, the sinful nature has built altars using these experiences and thus established thrones. These thrones give the external devils access to us through the door of our minds, which are opened by the sinful nature.

As a believer, although our spirit man is unaffected, the battle rages within our souls. The sinful nature knows that it is losing ground, so it does whatever is necessary to keep us in our history and locked up in our minds, with distorted images of ourselves, in order to keep the thrones established.

For example, you may have been a great worrier before your salvation experience. Being saved does not guarantee that you will no longer be classified by yourself or by others as a person who worries. Everything within your soulish area will act up and say to you, "You have a right to be very worried about a situation, because worrying is what you do and who you are."

Or perhaps you suffered from depression before your salvation experience. Afterward those feelings of depression may have intensified. Why? Your true identity is clouded by the voice of the sinful nature that says to you, "You are depressed. Depression is who you are."

Yet another example might be that you were abandoned by your parents in one way or another and the feeling of being an orphan has always plagued you. Even being born again has not changed the way you feel.

There are many more distorted images like these that the sinful nature uses to bombard your mind and release feelings of powerlessness within you. So you resign yourself to believing the lie that this is who you are. But buried deep within you, longing for an opportunity for expression, is your spirit man, whispering, "You are not your sinful nature and you are not your mind. You are spirit, made in the very image and likeness of God, empowered to conquer, dominate, and govern your circumstances."

The mind is the most powerful tool the enemy uses to gain access to our souls (see Rom. 8:5-17). The greatest battle we will ever fight is in our minds. The mind is located in the soul and acts as a control centre for our personalities. If our minds are not renewed and transformed (see Rom. 12:2), we can become slaves to them and by extension the sinful nature. This is the number one access or door satan uses into our lives facilitated by the sinful nature (see Rom. 8:5-17). Unless our minds are renewed (see Rom. 12:2), the sinful nature has the power to continue to give the enemy access. Ultimately any mind that is not renewed by the Spirit of God will be controlled by the sinful nature. The sinful nature gives instructions to the soul, and our behavior reflects such instructions and keeps gratifying the insatiable desires of the sinful nature. (See Galatians 5:17-23.) Therefore, when the enemy comes in and finds himself, he makes his abode within those compartments of our lives that have not been surrendered, and we walk a defeated life as children of God, never growing up into the fullness of our sonship.

The sinful nature uses the mind to communicate to us the lies that ensure we manifest the characteristics of its nature and provides an open door for demonic powers to gain entrance. For example, if someone says something negative to you, that thing will not have any effect on you unless you internalize it. If you internalize it, it becomes an ungodly belief that the sinful nature will use to keep you captive.

Let's say that as a born-again believer, the recorder starts to replay in your mind regarding your history and tells you that because of certain things that have happened to you, you have a right to walk in unforgiveness. If you empower the thought by embracing it, then the spirit of unforgiveness already alive and well within your sinful nature will continue to uphold that particular throne established within you. Forgiving will be the hardest thing for you to do.

Let's say you have a thought that you will always be in lack and your circumstances produce all the evidence needed to confirm that poverty is your only future regardless of what God has said. If you embrace that ungodly belief, the spirit of poverty lurking within your soulish area will continue to sit on the throne of that ungodly belief of poverty.

The point is, when we embrace ungodly beliefs that remove us from the truth of who we are in God and cause us to accept a lie, we open the door for the sinful nature to allow associated spirits to establish thrones within our beings. God desires truth in our innermost parts. Embracing lies will cause truth to be elusive to us. Never forget, satan's greatest desire is to destroy the image of God on the earth so that he can receive uninterrupted worship for himself. Refuse to be party to that!

We must understand this because the world looks on and wonders what the difference is between the believer and themselves. The only difference between the believer and the unbeliever is that the believer's spirit has been regenerated, while the unbeliever's spirit is still dead, paralyzed, and held captive by the enemy. Both have a soul, and both have a sinful nature. The believer has the inner power and strength to fight that nature, whereas the unbeliever does not. The believer has no excuse for operating like the unbeliever. The believer must come into the fullness of operating as a completely regenerated spirit being with a soul that lives in a body, walking in full dominion and authority, in order to give the unbeliever hope!

To explore this further, we will go back to our text in Jeremiah 1:10, which reads: *"See, today I appoint you over nations and kingdoms to uproot and tear down, to destroy and to overthrow, to build and to plant."* When applying this in context to our assignment on the earth, we must first apply it to ourselves.

Overthrowing the Kingdoms of Satan and Establishing the Kingdom of God

Every kingdom established in the earth that is contrary to the sovereign rule of God finds its root in the tree of the knowledge of good and evil and by extension satan himself. In the verse before, God commands Jeremiah to destroy and overthrow those kingdoms and rebuild and plant in the empty space left by their destruction by establishing God's Kingdom. Any time a stronghold is dethroned and the area is left void, another intruder stronger and more powerful than the one before comes in. It is extremely important not only to destroy the stronghold but also to immediately replace it with standards that establish the sovereign reign of God.

Let us now take this verse off the pages of the book and apply it to ourselves. We understand that the sinful nature is the seed of satan. Therefore, all kingdoms controlled by the sinful nature within our beings must be uprooted, dethroned, and torn down. This is where deliverance or the exorcism of demons and inner healing can be applied to our lives. Remember, Jesus said that when a strong man is cast out of a house (individual), it roams in arid places. It then comes back, finds that house clean, and invites others stronger than itself to occupy that house again. (See Matthew 12:43-45.) That strong man's assignment is to obtain legal access and secure his position in the earth realm through this house or individual by distorting the image of God.

Jeremiah 1:15-16 makes this clear: *"Their kings will come and set up their thrones in the entrance of the gates of Jerusalem; they will come against all her surrounding walls and against all the towns of Judah."*

Therefore, when we take a stand by acknowledging that the kingdoms within our being that have been established and controlled by the sinful nature must be dethroned, torn down, and destroyed, our next task is to secure our houses (temples) by ensuring that our spirit man is being built up by planting the Word of truth within us. We are to build and plant anything needed for the growth of our spirits, to fully identify with the God who is within us, within His temple.

ENDNOTE

1. Genesis 3:15: *"I will put enmity between you and the woman, and between your* [satan's] *seed and hers."*

Chapter 12

The Regulations of the Temple

This is the law of the temple: All the surrounding areas on top of the mountain will be holy. Such is the law of the temple (Ezekiel 43:12).

We have dealt with the soul and the controlling entity that governs the soulish area, namely the sinful nature, and the need for our spirits to regain dominance. Let us now address the body.

We discussed earlier that our bodies are the temple of the Holy Spirit or the Holy of Holies as referred to in the original translation. Ezekiel 43, verses 10-12, describe God's requirement for the temple:

*Son of man, describe the temple to the people of Israel, that they may be ashamed of their sins. Let them consider the plan, and if they are ashamed of all they have done, make known to them **the design of the temple**—its arrangement, its exits and entrances—its whole design and all its regulations and laws. Write these down before them so that they may be faithful to its design and follow its regulations. **This is the law of the temple: All the surrounding area on top of the mountain will be most holy. Such is the law of the temple.***

As children of God becoming sons of God, we must make a covenant with the Lord to keep the surrounding areas of His temple (our bodies) most holy. That means our eyes and what we see, our ears and what we listen to, our lips and what we entertain and therefore speak (for out of the abundance of the heart the mouth speaks) must be holy. In addition, our hands and what we touch, our feet and where we go, our hearts and what we hold dear to us (godly or ungodly beliefs, God or idols), our minds and what we meditate on, and our emotions and what we feed them (the area of the soul where our history becomes our reality) must also be holy.

Every square inch of the temple is being measured to ensure that it lines up to God's original specifications. God is a God of order as well as holiness. He states in Ezekiel 43:8: *"When they placed their threshold next to my threshold and their doorposts beside my doorposts with only a wall between me and them, they defiled my holy name by their detestable practices, so I destroyed them in my anger. Now let them put away from me their prostitution and the lifeless idols of their kings, and **I will live among them forever.**"*

THE BELIEVER AS THE TEMPLE OF GOD

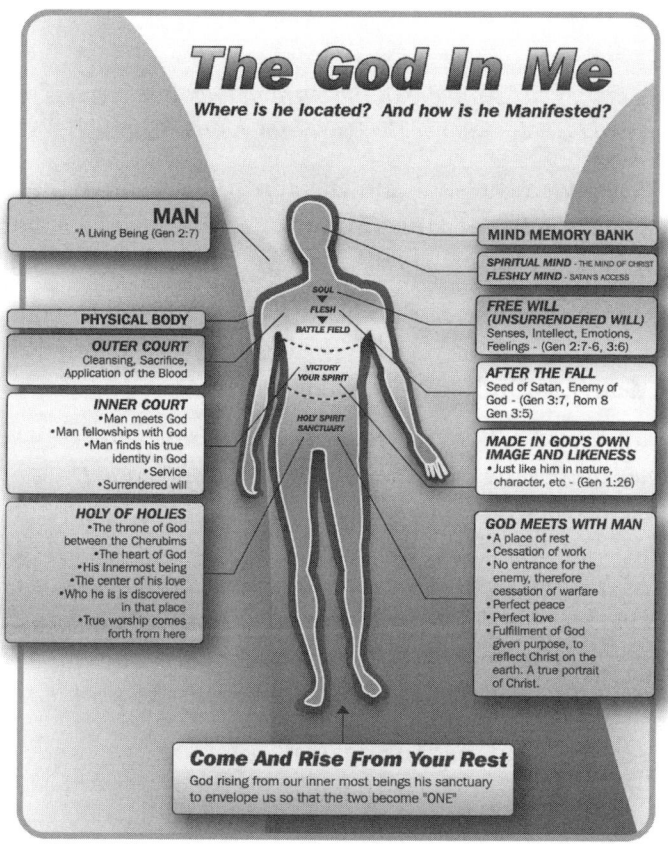

The God In Me
Where is he located? And how is he Manifested?

MAN
"A Living Being (Gen 2:7)

PHYSICAL BODY

OUTER COURT
Cleansing, Sacrifice, Application of the Blood

INNER COURT
• Man meets God
• Man fellowships with God
• Man finds his true identity in God
• Service
• Surrendered will

HOLY OF HOLIES
• The throne of God between the Cherubims
• The heart of God
• His Innermost being
• The center of his love
• Who he is is discovered in that place
• True worship comes forth from here

SOUL
FLESH
BATTLE FIELD
VICTORY
YOUR SPIRIT
HOLY SPIRIT
SANCTUARY

MIND MEMORY BANK
SPIRITUAL MIND - THE MIND OF CHRIST
FLESHLY MIND - SATAN'S ACCESS

FREE WILL (UNSURRENDERED WILL)
Senses, Intellect, Emotions, Feelings - (Gen 2:7-6, 3:6)

AFTER THE FALL
Seed of Satan, Enemy of God - (Gen 3:7, Rom 8 Gen 3:5)

MADE IN GOD'S OWN IMAGE AND LIKENESS
• Just like him in nature, character, etc - (Gen 1:26)

GOD MEETS WITH MAN
• A place of rest
• Cessation of work
• No entrance for the enemy, therefore cessation of warfare
• Perfect peace
• Perfect love
• Fulfillment of God given purpose, to reflect Christ on the earth. A true portrait of Christ.

Come And Rise From Your Rest
God rising from our inner most beings his sanctuary to envelope us so that the two become "ONE"

The layout of the body is a representation of the physical temple God is referring to in this Scripture. God never intended to continue to dwell in a building. His desire has always been to dwell within His people. Hence, Paul makes it clear that our bodies are the temple of the Holy Spirit who dwells within us. (See 1 Corinthians 6:19-20.) According to the layout of the physical temple, our spirit man is the Holy of Holies. Our soul is the inner court, and our physical body is the outer court.

THE OUTER COURT—THE PHYSICAL BODY

In the outer court, we find the brazen altar where sacrifices were made and the blood was applied, and the laver where washing took place. These two pieces of furniture represent our initial born-again experience—baptism and sanctification. These two experiences are outward expressions. (Our confession of Christ and our baptism are in most cases public confessions.)

THE INNER COURT—THE SOUL

In the inner court or holy place, we find the lampstand, which represents the revealed Word of God (*rhema*), and the table of shewbread, which represents fellowship with the Holy Spirit. In this place man meets God, man fellowships with God, man finds his true identity in God. This is the place where service comes out of relationship with God and not a need to be needed or to be useful or be seen. This place reveals a surrendered will. The work done in the life of the believer from this place is an inner working of the Holy Spirit and may not be seen immediately.

This is the place where the battle rages the most, because in this area of the soul is where the sinful nature has had a foothold and does everything possible to hinder the believer from experiencing and enjoying the benefits of being in the holy place. In this place, the believer can settle and delay the experience and satisfaction of dwelling in the next dimension, namely the Holy of Holies or man's spirit.

THE HOLY OF HOLIES—THE SPIRIT MAN

In the Holy of Holies, we find the golden altar of incense, which represents the fragrance of our communion with God through prayer and worship, and the golden ark of the covenant, which represents a face-to-face encounter with God. (The very presence of God dwelt above the mercy seat on the ark of the covenant.)[1] We also find the following within the ark of the covenant: the golden jar of manna, which represents a fresh revelation of who God is and reminds us of the angels surrounding the throne of God as they cry holy, holy, holy because of the fresh revelation of God they see every time they look at Him; Aaron's staff that budded, which represents our ordination by God Himself as we are released into our assignment; and the stone tablet of the covenant, which represents the written Word of God (His covenant and promises) as we come into full agreement with them (see Exod. 24:1-8).

This place is resident in our spirit man and in this place we find the establishment of the throne of God within us. We find the heart of God and we find the center of the love of God as we allow Him to walk us amidst the stones of fire[2] within Him. We discover who God is in that place and true worship comes forth from there.

In this place, God meets man and Spirit communicates with spirit. Deep calls unto deep. This is a place of rest, of cessation of work. There is no entrance for the enemy; therefore, there is cessation of inner conflicts and warfare. It is a place of perfect peace, where *Jehovah Shalom* becomes a reality. It is a place of perfect love, which is manifested in truth and light. In this place, God-given purpose is fulfilled, which is to reflect a true portrait of the Godhead in Christ on the earth. Accessing this place is the reason Christ died. This place is available to all those who are willing to take the journey to the end, and to see "there" as their ultimate goal and desire.

Jesus' death made access to this place possible and introducing us to Father is His greatest joy. The sinful nature has one assignment, which is to maintain the veil over our souls and spirits and keep this place hidden from our sight.

With the understanding of the layout of the temple as it relates to both the physical structure and our bodies, we can now put into context the word of the Lord in Ezekiel 42:8 that says, "*When they placed their threshold next to my threshold and their doorposts besides my doorposts with only a wall between me and them, they defile my holy name by their detestable practices.*"

Within the temple a veil or curtain separated the different dimensions of access to God. When our souls are corrupted by the sinful nature and we are controlled by that nature, we commit all manner of sinfulness against God. He is saying that He dwells within us and the distance between our soul and spirit is too close; therefore, we place our threshold next to His threshold and our doorpost next to His doorpost and defile His presence within us.

I am trying to paint a picture of the spiritual environment within our being. Can you visualize it? I reiterate, when we were saved and invited Jesus to come into our lives, He came through the person of the Holy Spirit and took up residence in the deep recesses of our spirit. The Holy Spirit enables and empowers us to crucify our sinful nature and renews and changes us daily into God's original design for His temple (a picture of perfection that is maturity in fulfilling purpose, wholeness, consistency, and completion).

While the Holy Spirit is in the deep recesses of our spirit and we continue to live lives that are unsanctified by yielding ourselves to the works of the sinful nature and not submitting ourselves to the Holy Spirit, then we invite the anger of God. God is not about to allow us to defile His holy name or subject Him to unholy practices. When His glory comes, His chastening comes with Him.

God's original intent for His temple, His dwelling place, is that we be well-balanced in our relationship with Him and with each other. He never intended for us to be in lack and dysfunctional. His design was complete unity and consistency in our relationship with Him, not lopsided in any way—strong in one area and weak in another. No way! The Lord has designed His temple to be a complete unit (see Exod. 26:1-6)[3], a complete unit walking in wholeness and consistency, fulfilling the purpose for which we agreed to come, giving Jesus the joy of the reward of His suffering by manifesting His true image and likeness in the earth realm.

Let us covenant with God to keep His temple holy within and without, for this is the law of the temple.

Endnotes

1. This is what Paul refers to in Hebrews 4:16: *"Let us approach the throne of grace with confidence, so that we may receive mercy and find grace to help us in our time of need."*

Introduction

THE JOURNEY OF BECOMING

So often as born-again believers we strive so hard to do! We want to help God, to be used by God, and to do things for Him. Ephesians 2 reminds us that God created us before the foundation of the earth to be co-laborers with Him to "do" good works.

The key word in this verse is *co-laborers*. The Oxford dictionary defines *co* as "joint, mutual, common, together or alike." Therefore, we were released in the earth realm to work together with God and not for God, and since it was God's decision to allow us to work with Him, then it stands to reason that He has the master plan and blueprint for the job, as well as the qualifications necessary for His co-laborers.

One of His first requirements is that we be formed into the image of His Son Jesus Christ, and right here is where the journey of "becoming" begins.

MY JOURNEY TO BECOMING

As a young believer, my one desire was to become all that Jesus died for, to be just like Him, and fulfill my purpose on the earth, so that when I stand before the Father on that "great day," I would hear resounding in Heaven the words, "*Well done good and faithful servant, enter into the joy of the Lord!*" (See Matthew 25:23.)

As time went by my passion and yearning for God intensified to the extent that I was saying to God, "All of You or nothing at all; total commitment to You or take me off the face of the earth." Every year the cry got more intense. Before I knew it, God started to grant me my request in an unusual way. I began going through the process of "becoming," which required formation on the inside and involved much distress, torment, and severe spiritual harassment. Severe spiritual battles continued in my life for a period of more than four years. During this time the power and presence of God were very real to me, very tangible. I felt that He wore me as an outer garment and I wore Him as my inner garment.

Although His presence was so tangible, there were many days and nights that I cried out for the journey to come to an end. I cried for closure (as I called it) to come, not recognizing that all of that was an answer to prayer. I tried everything possible to get out of the nightmare, until one day God revealed that He was in the midst of this thing mightily. I then decided to stop fighting and rest. I requested prayer for grace rather than escape! Why? The grace of God that God said to Paul is sufficient for him, really means "to rejoice, or joy, acceptance, favor, absolute freeness of the loving-kindness of God to men, finding its only motive in the bounty and freeheartedness of the Giver (God)."[1] In other words, the grace of God is a release of the joy of the Lord within, which is ultimately our strength, to go through anything and come out without the smell of smoke.[2] I remembered saying to a friend, "If this is what it takes for the fullness of God to be made manifest in the earth in this body, so be it." This statement was confirmed when God made a personal visitation to me and a few friends at a hotel in Pensacola, Florida, in 2001 and pervaded my being with His person for hours. That experience made it very clear to me that I was just a body prepared for the Christ through the power of the Holy Spirit.

Today I look back at the four years of hell (in a real sense) I experienced, and while I would not wish it on my worst enemy, I thank God for walking with me and in me through the valley of death and causing me to fear no evil, but instead to bask in His love for me that knows no boundaries or limitations. I thank Him for trusting me with Himself

Introduction

and allowing me to face the very hordes of hell just as He did, and to rise again in His power and deliverance. Most of all, I thank Him for allowing me to partake of the table He prepared before me in the presence of my enemies. (Please note that these enemies are not flesh and blood, but principalities and powers in dark and high places.)

You might be wondering what this experience was. Suffice it to say, whatever you will have to experience in order to "become," the end result is the fullness of the Godhead (Father, Son, and Holy Spirit) working and operating in your innermost being and an awareness of Him who is indescribably glorious and priceless. You will not want to miss this journey!

THE WILDERNESS EXPERIENCE

Every believer on the journey will sooner or later encounter the wilderness experience. Many believers have forfeited their inheritance at this stage of the journey because they mistakenly thought they had been forsaken by the Lord rather than this being "a calling away unto Himself."

The glamour and glory of the presence of God in a specific atmosphere can cause the believer to worship the atmosphere and the feelings it creates rather than pursue the person of the presence. A wilderness experience will certainly take care of that!

On the journey to sonship, we will discover that the wilderness is an important transition to ensure the completion of the journey, because it is a place where we shed the old and embrace the new. In the wilderness, old lovers are exposed and a new and pure betrothal takes place. In that experience, our roaming eyes become single.

There are many reasons for the wilderness. For example, the children of Israel were led into the wilderness to avoid heavy warfare that might have caused them to go running back to Egypt. Jesus was led into the desert (wilderness) to be tempted by the devil that He might come forth in the fullness of the Spirit.

Ultimately God leads us into the wilderness, or what we term "a dry place," to betroth us to Himself. Every true believer and pursuer of the person and presence of the Godhead will encounter a wilderness experience. It is a place where only God can provide water for the thirsting of the soul. King David cried out in Psalm 130:5-6, "*I wait for the Lord, my soul waits and in his word I put my hope. My soul waits for the Lord more than watchmen wait for the morning."*

In Psalm 63:1, 42:1-2, David says, *"O God, you are my God, earnestly I seek you; my soul thirsts for you, my body longs for you, in a dry and weary land where there is no water. As the deer pants for the water, so my soul pants for you. My soul thirsts for God, for the living God."*

When God reveals Himself, David says, *"I have seen you in the sanctuary and beheld your power and your glory because your love is better than life, my lips will glorify you."* Hallelujah!

This kind of experience is not for the fainthearted, but for the pursuers of God. It is for the God-chasers. It is for those who will forsake all for the person and presence of God, in order to live in His presence, walk within Him and have Him walk within them, gaze at His face, eat from His lips, and live in His being, where Heaven becomes the most natural place. It is where the believer aches for God and gets homesick outside of His presence. Any believer who seeks God for His face (who He is) and not His hands (what He can do) will encounter a wilderness experience.

The purpose of this experience is to create a hunger and thirst for God that no one and nothing but God can satisfy and create a chasm between our past life and newness in God. In Hosea 2 we get some insights into the results of a wilderness experience. They are:

1. The voice of the Spirit of God can be heard more clearly and tenderly.

2. What was once considered trouble takes a new perspective as hope.

3. The emergence of a new level of worship.

4. The emergence of a new level of intimacy. Jesus will no longer be seen only as Savior and Master but also as "my Husband."

5. All former lovers (anything attached to the believer that took the place of God) are removed.

6. The Father betroths us to Jesus forever in righteousness, justice, love, and compassion.

7. God plants us in Himself, and as He does that, Heaven finds agreement on the earth, and the earth of our beings

Introduction

will respond to Heaven and produce the joy and life of Heaven in our atmosphere.

God looks for a cry from within us that says "I want and need You more that life itself!"

MY WILDERNESS EXPERIENCE

When I first encountered this Scripture in Hosea, I thought, *My, what a great Word this would be to the Body*. I never imagined that this had anything to do with me personally. Within two years of encountering this Scripture, I entered into a wilderness experience that lasted one full year. I cried out to God day and night like David says he did in Psalm 63:1, *"My soul thirsts for you, my body longs for you, in a dry and weary land."* "Lord, where are You? I cannot feel You. Where is my song? My mouth is dry. Where is my prayer and intercession, not a word to be uttered from my lips? Where is the life of Your Word?"

The heavens felt like brass. I said to God, "I would rather die than live without Your presence and the ability to worship." Then one day, after explaining what was happening to me to my mentor, she said these words, which I have never forgotten: "God is not about feelings. He wants you to know that He is present whether you feel Him or not." Those words changed my life and strategy. I stopped trying to feel and allowed myself to "be" in His presence in the wilderness.

The next season of wilderness came a few years after that experience. In 1998, I visited the Brownsville outpouring in Pensacola, Florida. While there I had a blood transfusion of the presence of the Lord. The Spirit of the Lord pervaded my life with such intensity that for many days I thought I would explode. The atmosphere of Heaven sat in my prayer room as the Holy Spirit took me into realms of the glory of God. Indeed the heavens were opened. I went from worshipping from my lips to the heart of God to accessing the life of the Spirit of God within me and communing Spirit to spirit for hours. My entire life took on new meaning. I lived just to be in the presence of Jesus, just to eat from the mouth of *Abba*. Fellowship and communion were my daily bread. There were days when I felt homesick for Heaven and did not want to remain in the earth realm.

Imagine right in the middle of all that, I entered into another wilderness experience. This time it was for a shorter period. Instead of experiencing the presence of God at home in my prayer room, I encountered Him only among believers at the height and intensity of great worship. At home He was nowhere to be felt or found. Pauline, my mentor's, words echoed again on the inside of me, "*God is not about feelings. He wants you to know that He is present whether you feel Him or not.*"

Then one morning the purpose for this wilderness experience was revealed. While in prayer, not feeling His presence, I heard myself utter these words, "Lord, I am tired of a one-night-stand relationship. I want to be committed to You in marriage." The Holy Spirit began to explain to me the prayer He had led me to pray. He explained that it is possible to be in love with the feeling that is created by His tangible glory upon me, the euphoria (ecstasy, joy, rapture, exhilaration, excitement) that envelops me, and still miss the fullness of a real relationship with Him, a relationship that demands total surrender to Him at any cost, a relationship that allows me to give myself over completely as a covenant Bride and settles the issue of His Lordship in every situation. As I said, "I do!" the Spirit of God broke through in my life once again, this time creating a chasm between my past life and desires and my new covenant relationship with the Godhead.

These two stages in the process of my formation prepared me for a greater level of becoming. Remember these words as you continue on the journey as a God-chaser. They will change you as they did me. "God is not about feelings. He wants you to know that He is present whether you feel Him or not."

Praise the Lord!

Endnotes

1. *Lexical Aid to The New Testament*, from *The Hebrew Greek Key Study Bible, from King James Version* (Chattanooga, TN: AMG International Inc. D/B/A Publishers, 1991), #5485.

2. In Daniel 3:19-26, we see the three Hebrew boys walking amidst the stones of fire within the very heart of God, when the king issued the order to have the fiery furnace turned up seven times hotter, because of their confession

of the God they served. "*O King Nebukanazzar we do not have to defend our position to you, the God we serve is able to save us, and He will save us. But even if He does not, we will not worship your idols.*" The moment that confession was made, they were immediately transferred from the natural realm to the supernatural realm, because of their agreement with Heaven. Entering the furnace was actually entering into the consuming fire of the love of God. They were among the fiery stones which is the center of the heart of God: His fiery, all-consuming, explosive love that destroys fear and breaks every chain of captivity. Their clothes never even smelt of smoke because of where they were positioned…in a realm called "LOVE." The greater the fire, the greater the manifestation of the love of God. We will never know that Love until we trust ourselves with Love to go through the fire, knowing that it will consume us but not destroy us. Our God is a consuming fire; therefore the consummation is really in Him.

Remember there will always be three stages of this process:

- Stage 1: The unknown: We do not understand what is happening.
- Stage 2: We start to handle what is happening to us in the flesh (or in our own strength).
- Stage 3: By our confession (surrendered will) or our agreement with the "will" of Heaven, we take our final step into the supernatural provision and love of God.

Chapter 13

God Chastens Those He Loves

My son, do not make light of the Lord's discipline, and do not lose heart when he rebukes you, because the Lord disciplines those he loves, and he punishes everyone he accepts as a son (Hebrews 12:5-6).

What does *process* mean? Is process of God or of the enemy? Is it normal or abnormal? Is there purpose in process? How long is the process? These are the many questions believers ask or think of when the word *process* is mentioned. The writer of Hebrews gives us some insight into these questions by revealing to us the heart of the Father in this regard.

The literal translation of our opening verse reads this way: *"For whom the Lord loves, He disciplines, and whips every son whom He receives."* Verse 8 continues by making it even clearer: *"But if you are without discipline, of which all have become sharers, then you are bastards and not sons."* In other words, if we are not chastened by God, then we become illegitimate children.

The words "He disciplines" speak to us of "bringing up a child, to educate." They are used to describe activities directed toward the moral and spiritual nurture and training of a child, to influence conscious will and action, or to instruct or chastise in order to educate someone to conform to divine truth.[1]

The mark of a true son is to identify with his father. God's chastening is to enable us to look like Him at the end of the journey, in order to take hold of our inheritance. You might ask at this point, "Why should I go through anymore than I have already gone through?" Remember the things you went through came about as a result of the canal of sin you passed through when you made the journey to the earth. The chastening of God is to remove the distorted images created by that canal and bring into focus His true image and our likeness to Him. His chastening is to remove all the dross[2] that attached itself to us as we lived under the influence of sin.

There are many believers sitting in churches today who do not know how or refuse to give themselves over to Father for chastening. They are either fearful or downright unwilling to go through the process of formation. They stand afar, taking the stance of an illegitimate child who does not have an inheritance to possess. At the same time, they criticize those who accept the fact that they are legitimate children and, as such, are aware of the Father's legitimacy in chastening them so they can partake of the fullness of their inheritance in Christ in the Father.

The prodigal son knew that he was legitimate, and as a result, understood he had an inheritance and a right to it. He was confident about asking for his inheritance, although his motives and timing may have been off, because he understood the inheritance was already his. When asked, his father did not dispute his claim and gave him what had been allotted to him.

The pain of his bad timing and poor choices caused him to return to the house of his father. He not only understood the nature of his inheritance but also the depths of his father's love for him. He knew what would move his father's heart—a humble and contrite spirit, the act of repentance, acknowledging his failings and weaknesses, and submitting to the will of his father.

The prodigal's brother, on the other hand, lived in the house of the father all his life, and yet he never knew his father's heart. He lived with the father in the same house, but never embraced the bosom of his father. He never did anything questionable and was fully committed to being a hard worker on the father's estate. Still he behaved like a servant rather than a son. He never embraced his inheritance. It was his to have, yet he did not think he had a right to it. So when his father threw a party to celebrate his brother's homecoming, he complained about a fattened calf, and a robe, and a ring—all of which were available to him as well.

The prodigal's brother complained about his hard work and years of commitment and the fact that in his eyes he was never celebrated. His words are a true sign of a heart that has embraced a spirit of illegitimacy. He lived afar like most of us and never released himself or let his guard down to become a son to the father. He remained locked into *doing* rather than *being* in the hope that he would be accepted and rewarded for what he did and not for who he had become in the father.

This scenario is typical in the Body of Jesus Christ today. Believers are taught to "do" and not to "be" and as a result, they are constantly seeking to do more as a requirement for coming into the fullness of the pleasure of the Father (in other words, for acceptance).

This lie has its roots in the tree of the knowledge of good and evil, which entices believers to jostle for positions that enable them to be seen and deceives them into believing the more they are seen and accepted by man and man-made systems, the more they are recognized by God. As this happens, Jesus sits back, sadly watches, and quietly whispers, "Your fixed position is 'in' Me 'in' the Father. I already paid the price. My yoke is easy and my burden is light. You are a co-laborer, and as a co-laborer you are also coheirs of all that the Father has given Me ownership of, which is *everything*."

God understands the process that each of us needs in order to bring us to the place of submitting to His chastening—chastening that will ultimately result in our formation as sons. He will allow us in some instances to take what we perceive as our freedom, which is to "long after the food of pigs" (as the prodigal son did), knowing that that kind of process is what necessary to release a yes from our innermost beings to begin the process of formation of the fullness of His image within us. The father of the prodigal understood what his son needed and released him, knowing that the chastening would accomplish its perfect work.

We must always remember that God's chastening is to reveal to us what is present within us empowering the sinful nature. The Lord knows the heart of man; therefore, He does not need to prove anything to Himself. He will allow the chastening so that we can seek His face and allow Him to change us from one level of glory to another. If He allows us to stay where we are, we will become stagnant and be delayed in our growing up as sons.

Wherever we are on this journey, our only option is to say yes to the chastening, in whatever form God determines.

Come on in. Don't linger at the gate. Only beggars stay at the gate. It is your Father's pleasure to give you the Kingdom (see Luke 12:32).

Endnotes

1. *Lexical Aid to the New Testament,* from *The Hebrew Greek Key Study Bible, from King James Version* (Chattanooga, TN: AMG International Inc. D/B/A Publishers, 1991), #381.

2. Impurities—the rubbish that separates us from the true character and nature of God within us.

Chapter 14

It Is Time to Be Healed

Therefore, strengthen your feeble arms and weak knees. Make level paths for your feet, so that the lame may not be disabled, but rather healed (Hebrews 12:12-13).

The twelfth chapter of Hebrews continues from the eleventh as the Holy Spirit invites us to take a look at the sufferings of those who went on before us, the ones He describes as the "cloud of witnesses." He gives us a glimpse into the heavenlies that assures us we are not taking this journey alone. In the corridors of Heaven, looking down are witnesses who have suffered to the point of death as described in chapter 11—now they are busy cheering us on. These godly witnesses in Hebrews 12:1 are encouraging us to *"lay aside every weight and the easily surrounding sin, and to run the race set before us with patience"* (Literal Translation).

They tell us to look to "the author and finisher of our faith, Jesus, who for the joy set before Him, endured the cross, having despised the shame, and sat down at the right hand of the throne of God, where we also sit with Him and in Him." (Author's paraphrase.)

After we have been told all of this, we are encouraged to embrace the chastening of the Father so that we can embrace the truth that "it is time to be healed" and not to remain lame, whether in our emotions, mind, or even our bodies, but to be formed into the fullness of the full measure of Christ.

THE RIGHT TO BE FORMED

What Is Formation and What Does It Look Like?

The key factor in understanding the process is to recognize that we must "become" before we "do." The opposite has occurred, and as a result many believers are so trapped in the busyness of ministry, church, and work that they are afraid to stop *doing* and just *be*. In some cases, they are too afraid to stop long enough because they want to turn a deaf ear to the voices within crying out to be healed. *Doing* keeps the believer looking outside self, while *being* brings the believer to a higher dimension of an internal focus of the inward workings of the presence of God within (see Ps. 91:1-2). For some this concept sounds like a foreign language.

The opposite of rest is *busyness* (reserved only for the wicked) and is translated in God's vocabulary as "for the wicked like the sea driven, unable to be quiet and whose waters cast up mire and mud" (Isaiah 57:20-21). (Author's paraphrase.) The word *driven* in this verse speaks of "being driven out from a possession." In other words, when we are driven by activity, we are driven further and further away from possessing our inheritance, which is found in the fullness of the rest of God. We are unable to overcome and endure. We become powerless, unable to prevail or keep still and unable to endure any major form of suffering because we have not been able to possess the rest of God, which gives us strength and brings us to a place of wholeness. The main strategy of the enemy is to keep us so busy and distracted that although we have entered the promised land through the blood of Jesus, we are unable to possess the fullness and richness of our inheritance in Christ, struggling to take hold of what is the most natural thing for us to have. This struggle eventually results in frustration and hopelessness.

Coming into the "rest" of God is the ultimate for the believer. The Israelites were unable to enter the "rest" of God because of unbelief. We have been unable to enter because we do not believe what the Word of God has to say about us. King David in 1 Chronicles 23:25-26 endorsed the "rest" of God by relieving the Levites (responsible for carrying the ark of the covenant and taking care of the furnishings of the tabernacle) from *doing* to *being*. He told them, *"Since the Lord, the God of Israel, has granted rest to His people and has come to dwell in Jerusalem forever, the Levites no longer need to carry the tabernacle or any of the articles used in its service."*

The "carry" we need to carry is the glory of the Lord in us and through us. Only when we find that place of rest within God can He find a place of rest within us to allow Him to fulfill His purpose in the earth unhindered through His Body. That is what brings pleasure to God—not our works. Our mode of operation must change. We have placed the cart before the horse for too long. There is a prescribed way to operate and function in the Kingdom of God. God Himself set it up, and He will only respond to His Way, not man's way.

The process of *becoming* is where we find true healing. In that process, God removes the mask and debris and reveals the true treasure hidden on the inside. I am convinced that the concept of *doing* before *becoming* came as a deception to cause believers to rely on "works," separating us from the joy of becoming and resting in the work of the Father. His work, by the way, is creative and artistic, never tiresome or burdensome.

For the believer to become, Christ must be formed in him or her. Paul expressed this very well when he said to the Galatians, *"My little children, for whom I am again suffering birth pangs until Christ is completely and permanently formed (molded) within you"* (Galatians 4:19 AMP). The Oxford dictionary defines *form* as the "mode in which a thing exists or manifests itself." The Strong's Greek dictionary defines *form* from two words meaning "to fashion through the idea of adjustment or parts, shape (figuratively speaking: nature)," and also as "a part, to get as a section of allotment, a share of."

In other words, *to be formed* carries the meaning of "being fashioned by way of adjustment and shape, as well as being part of, or sharing a part of something or someone" in this instance. Our share is to fully partake of our inheritance in Christ. God has so designed this that we cannot make it happen through the avenue of works, but only through the process of being fashioned, as our definitions make clear.

God's ideal for believers is for us to allow Him to take us through the process of formation. Not transformation, which is the end result of being formed, but rather formation out of nothing. The Oxford dictionary defines *transformation* as "the outward appearance, character, and disposition." The outward appearance of the caterpillar is a butterfly, but the metamorphosis takes place inwardly.

The alternative words used for *form* are "configuration, makeup, anatomy, constitution, inner form, essence, substance." Additional meanings are the action words "cut out, carve, chisel, sculpture, knit, weave, hammer out, punch out, create, construct, bring into being and knock into shape."[1]

From the above listing, it is very clear that the process of becoming can and will be a painful but satisfying experience. Our configuration must be changed from the distorted ungodly beliefs of our past experiences. Our makeup must be changed from body, soul, and spirit, to spirit, soul, and body, where spirit rules. Our constitution (rules and laws that govern us) must be in full agreement with the heartbeat of Heaven as written in the Word of God, without question. Inwardly, our inner man (spirit man) must become stronger. We must become a people of substance and the very essence of Heaven must be formed within our beings.

The process will take place as the Holy Spirit begins to cut out, hammer out, punch out, and chisel out anything that is hindering Christ from being fully formed in the believer. The normal thing to do is to run from the process and ask the questions, "Why?" and "When?" My encouragement to the believer is to stay in the process. After the hindrances are removed, the process of carving and sculpting, knitting, weaving, constructing, and recreating His image and character in the believer begins. His aim is to bring us into being by knocking us into shape.

This process requires the believer's time and commitment. The time necessary for the working out of this process does not start with the crowd, but rather in the believer's quiet time before the Godhead on a daily basis. For many believers the wounds and ungodly beliefs they carry are so deep that formation will take time, as much time as their degree of willingness to surrender completely to the scalpel of the Chief Physician.

As we continue on this journey, commitment to healing and wholeness and coming into the Shalom of God, where there is nothing missing or broken, is a requirement for obtaining our inheritance. Our commitment is to a surrendered will that whispers like Mary, "Be it unto me according to Your word"—according to what gives Heaven pleasure, according to what will cause the manifest presence of God to be seen, known, and correctly interpreted in the earth realm in and through our beings, regardless of what it will cost our flesh!

This point of the journey is where the wings of the Spirit of God open up to cover us from the distracting attacks of the enemy or the noisome pestilences (see Ps. 91). The vultures will encounter the Holy Spirit, since the battle becomes the Lord's and not ours. It is important to understand that the battle is between satan and the image of God within us, who is Jesus Christ Himself. He has already won the battle and given us the victory.

For many believers, although the battle has been won and they are winning small external conflicts, they lose the war waged on the inside. Let us not shortchange ourselves by settling for less than the reward of the sufferings of Christ. Go ahead! Say yes to a surrendered will! It is your right!

Endnote

1. *New Lexicon Webster's Dictionary* (New York, NY: Lexicon Publication Inc., 1987).

Chapter 15

Time to Possess

Now since the Lord, the God of Israel has driven the Amorites out before His people Israel, what right have you to take it over? Will you not take what your god Chemosh gives you? Likewise, whatever the Lord our God has given to us we will possess (Judges 11:23-24).

We will now embark on another dimension of the journey—the part that incorporates our relationship with the Body of Jesus Christ and the marketplace. I pray that your passion for God has been stirred and you have grasped the understanding of your true nature and origin. I pray that you understand that the Kingdom of God is within you and so your fixed position is in the bosom of the Father, sitting in heavenly places in Christ Jesus. There is an inheritance to possess, and you will possess it regardless of the cost. Jesus will indeed have the reward of His suffering.

In concluding this section of the journey, I want to highlight a very interesting character in Judges 11. His name is Jephthah, and he is described as a mighty warrior or a man of valor (strength and courage). We know he was a Gileadite because his father's name was Gilead. His mother's name is unknown but her occupation was given as a prostitute. Yes, Jephthah was the son of a prostitute. He grew up with his stepmother and half-brothers, but as he grew older, he was driven out and disinherited by his siblings. He was rejected and disowned.

His siblings told him that he had no right to his inheritance by saying in Judges 11:2, *"You are not going to get any inheritance in our family because you are the son of another woman"* (prostitute). They had forgotten that it was not the blood of another woman in his veins but the blood of Gilead, his father. He had as much right to his inheritance—even more right than his siblings, since he was the firstborn and the blessings of the firstborn belonged to him. Talk about being disenfranchised! Even so, Jephthah left without a fight. When you know whose you are, fighting to establish your identity is out of the question. The day of reckoning always comes and the opportunity is then seized. Jephthah fled to the land of Tob, where like attracted like and he became the leader of a group of adventurers and outcasts.

Some time later, Israel found itself continuously embroiled in battle with its enemies. They never *fully possessed the land that had been given to them*, and what had been left unconquered came back to mock, haunt, hunt, and terrorize them. Their enemies continued to destroy everything they tried to build. That is exactly what happens when we do not possess our inheritance and allow the Spirit of God to make room so that Christ can be formed on the inside. The enemy seizes the opportunity and comes to us and says, "You had your opportunity to keep me in the defeated position but you failed to possess. A crack was left and I infiltrated and made it twice as hard as it was before." Many believers have and are experiencing this kind of mockery and infiltration after their born-again experience.

Israel, once again exposed, was in need of a leader to take them into battle against their enemies. Who among them did God say was a mighty warrior, a leader of strength and courage? Looking around, they could not find anyone. Then, the elders of Israel remembered Jephthah. There was no question about it that he was a mighty warrior. Now in need, they cared little that he was the son of a prostitute and unworthy to share the inheritance from his father.

The potential of God within us, which is the identity of God Himself, can never be destroyed. The seed of the Word of God can be dormant within us temporarily, but the life of God applied to it will always cause it to germinate again and spring forth. God's Word becomes alive on the inside of us whenever agreement can be found. If the seed and the soil have no agreement, it really does not matter how much rain falls or sun shines—the seed will not grow. In other words, it does not matter how much oil is poured upon the believer to walk in his or her inheritance; without agreement that experience will not produce any lasting fruit.

In the book of Hosea 2:21-22, we read, " *'In that day, I will respond,' declares the Lord—'I will respond to the skies, and they will respond to the earth; and the earth will respond to the grain, the new wine and oil, and they will respond to Jezreel* (God plants).' "

This is agreement. The key to all of this is to ensure that there is agreement with the Spirit of Almighty God. The facts might be clearly defined, but truth supersedes facts. Stick to truth and possess your inheritance.

Going back to Jephthah, we notice that he knew who he was and whose he was. He was never controlled by the opinions of others. He knew he was a mighty warrior, born to lead, and he never allowed anyone or anything— not his environment, circumstances, background, his brothers, or his parental code—to shape his world or carve out his reality or identity. He saw himself exactly the way God saw him—as a mighty warrior and leader, a man of might and power, strength and ability, wealth and substance. He never wavered from that. His worth was sealed and *fully formed on the inside of him!* He chose to possess his inheritance.

When he was approached by the elders of Israel, he seized the opportunity for which he had waited. He had decided a long time before that he was not going to fight with his brothers over his birthright, property, or identity. He understood that encoded in his name[1] was the process of formation, a process that would cause him to be naked or exposed and yet feel no shame. Though ploughed or carved, he knew when he emerged, engraved within his resolve was the God-given ability to loosen, break forth, and draw out any hindrance in his path without reducing himself to the level of the enemy. He knew that wealth was on the inside of him. All he needed was resident on the inside of him, and in due season when he needed access to what was resident on the inside, he just reached in and all was well.

Understanding all that, he knew beyond a shadow of a doubt that he was the man for the job. He responded to the elders by saying, "Suppose you take me back to fight the Ammonites and the Lord gives them to me. Will I really be your leader?" (Judges 11:9). (Author's paraphrase.)

The enemy knows who you are and whose you are! His strategy is to make sure you never possess your inheritance. The choice is yours.

Jephthah, now the leader of the tribe of Gilead, takes matters in hand and sends a message to the leader of the Ammonite army, seeking to understand the reason for the attack on Israel. He is dealing with this situation with a level head, very much in command. What a comeback! The king of the Ammonites responds in Judges 11:13 by saying, *"When Israel came up out of Egypt, they took away my land from the Arnon to the Jabbok, all the way to the Jordan. Now give it back peaceably."* (See Numbers 21:24.)

The remainder of this chapter makes it very clear that the Ammonites were not the original landowners—the Amorites were. Three hundred years after the fact, the king of the Ammonites was demanding the return of something that never belonged to him.

The audacity of the enemy! He will disguise himself as the possessor of our souls when he is nothing other than a squatter.[2] We are God's property, His inheritance purchased by the blood of His Son before the creation of the world, made in His own image and after His likeness, birthed out of His heart, mind, and mouth (the breath of God). Yet, because of the sin sickness, the enemy took up residence in the land (the body that houses the very nature and image of God), and refuses to move. He will do anything to remain there, and *we are peaceably giving in!*

How did this awesome dialogue between Jephthah and the enemy end? This is the conclusion of the matter and the conclusion of the journey to sonship, taken from Judges 11:23, *"Since the Lord, the God of Israel, has driven the Amorites out before his people Israel, what right have you to take it over? Will you not take what your god Chemosh gives you? Likewise, whatever the Lord our God has given to us we will possess."*

Hallelujah. I am about to explode!

Those words continue to resound from the heart of God to us today: "What have I given to you to possess? It is time to possess your inheritance":

- Time to possess the revelation of who you are and evict the squatter. (See endnote for note on *squatter*.)

- Time to possess the revelation of who you are in God and who He is in you.

- Time to possess the revelation of the finished work of Calvary. It is "finished; it stands finished; and it always will be finished."[3]

- Time to possess the revelation of the power of the resurrection, the same power that is resident on the inside of you to allow the fullness of the Godhead to be manifested in such a glorious way that Christ will be seen, known, and correctly interpreted.

- Time to possess the resurrection power of the Holy Spirit that causes you to be more than a conqueror, with enough backbone to withstand any and all attacks of the enemy. Why? Because we are hid in Christ in God. The battle is the Lord's! He has the power to keep you hidden in His heart so your perspective changes as you see things from His vantage point.

- Time to possess the revelation that "now are you a son of God" with the Father's DNA flowing through your veins and a mandate to increase and bear much fruit and reproduce sons (both genders).

- Time to possess God's creative power and ability within you, which defies settling for anything less than God's best, that speaks in full agreement and confidence, the will of God in the earth and in our circumstances. This power ensures that the Kingdom of God will be first established on the inside of us and then be seen by those around us.

Let us say like Paul, *"I want to know Christ and the power of his resurrection and the fellowship of sharing in his sufferings, becoming like him in his death, and so, somehow, to attain to the resurrection from the dead"* (Philippians 3:10-11).

In sharing in the fellowship of Christ's suffering, there will be testings and trials (which I call formation). The reason for this, as mentioned before, is that we live in a sin-sick world, and the flesh (sinful nature) must be conquered in order for us to be made whole. The victory has already been won. We just need to manifest it from the inside out. The way we handle circumstances externally is a clear indication of the atmosphere within us. God will not handle our external circumstances before He first perfects (matures, brings to completion) Himself on the inside of us, so that His life flows to the external circumstances from within and speaks His divine will to it.

In other words, our victories in our circumstances and attitudes are a reflection of the God that is within us. Let us stop the grumbling and complaining. Let us stop looking for a quick microwave fix and realize that greater is He that is in us than he that is in the world. Access, possess the God in you.

In days of old, God manifested His power and presence in a physical form, but in this hour He is manifested from within us. The victory of our circumstances is just a mirror image of the power at work within us.

Remember that you are a living, speaking spirit, birthed out of the heart, mind, and mouth of God with the power to create just as God did. His DNA flows through the very fabric of your being, giving life to His image, likeness, nature, and character within you. You are filled with the full measure of all the fullness of God; therefore, you are filled with God. Allow Him to stretch Himself within you.

Lack or ungodliness of any kind does not possess you, for you are fully possessed and conquered by the life of the Spirit of God within you.

It is time to access the God within you. It is time to be healed and made whole through the process of chastening and formation. Whatever our God has given to us, we will possess!

Endnotes

1. Jephthah in the original language means "he will open" (#3316) and comes from the prim. root #6605, which means "to open wide, (literally or figuratively) to loosen, begin, plough, carve: appear, break forth, draw out, engrave, unstop."

2. Squatters are anything in our belief system (distorted images) that are contrary to who God is and who He says that we are. Squatters are ungodly beliefs that have formed our identity based on our environment, background, and past experience.

Fear, unbelief, doubt, low self-esteem, lack of self-worth, lack of confidence, conflicting value systems (confessing one thing and doing another). An inability to receive love and return love—the love of God first, love for yourself, and then the love of others.

These squatters take up a position within the soulish area of our being, refusing to leave, because they believe that they have legal access. Instead of driving the squatters out, we find ourselves living among them to avoid conflict. To live among the squatters means to live in the fleshly/soulish area of our being, living way below the standard God has designed for us, and as a result unable to access the Spirit of God within us, to lift our spirit into the dominant position it should have. When the squatters in our internal landscape are evicted, then we will be in a position to apply the power of the presence of God within us to any external circumstances. Why? Because we are now operating in truth, we know whose we are and who we are. We are possessing our inheritance and will resist (oppose, refuse to accept, defy, stand firm against) any contrary or familiar spirits that come near our possession, whether it be our emotion, will, children, family, material possessions. We will stand up with our faces like flint, with a resounding no, saying, "We will possess what our God has given to us!"

3. Jesus' seven last words from the Greek translation of the word *tetelestai*. Warren W. Wiersbe, *Jesus' Seven Last Words* (Lincoln, NE: Back To The Bible, 1981), 58.

SECTION IV

Encounters on the Journey

"May Jesus Be Seen, Known, and Correctly Interpreted."

Introduction

In the previous section of this book, we dealt with our inheritance and the need to recognize that it is indeed time to take possession of it. As we answer the call and embrace fully what we have been given, sealed in the covenant of blood, we will discover that this inheritance embodies not just our relationship at new dimensions with the Godhead, but also the covenant He has with His entire Body, of which we are a part, as well as the inheritance He has given to us in the wider populace of peoples, tribes, and tongues in our communities and specifically in the marketplace. As we journey to full sonship, we will have the pleasure of discovering and experiencing divine encounters. We must begin this aspect of the journey with our encounter with the Body of Christ, so that we will have a clear understanding of the many members that embody who we are.

The Body of Christ

One of the main hindrances on the journey to full sonship is the distraction caused by our misunderstanding of our relationship with the Body of Jesus Christ. A body divided has a weak immune system that is unable to identify the subtle, hostile influences invading it. One reason the weakened body fails to recognize the deception of these influences is that they have taken up a form resembling the cells of the body. Take the AIDS virus, for example. It quite effectively does its destructive work by entering the body, duplicating the cells of the immune system, and mutating itself so that the immune system is unable to recognize it as an enemy. Eventually those duplicated cells attack the immune system, rendering it powerless to fight back.[1]

This same type of infiltration takes place in the Body of Christ simply because of a lack of understanding that we are indeed a body; and more importantly, the Body of Christ here on the earth with many members, cells, ligaments, and joints, all of which play an active role in its nourishment, growth, and development. When the understanding that we are the Body of Christ is fully embraced rather than just verbalized, each member takes an active role in upholding the Body by individually ensuring that we will only expose our cells to what is wholesome and beneficial to the greater good and development of the Body. In other words, we embrace our individual bodies as the temples of the Holy Spirit.

In this section we will focus on the makeup of the Body and its various functions. We will also learn what role those functions play in our individual, yet collective, growth in the manifestation of the image of God within us as His Body and sons of God.

Endnote

1. The specific target of retroviruses is the immune system, and that is what makes this kind of virus so deadly. Dr. Haseltine of Harvard said: "Once the infection is in, the damage has been done" (Haseltine, 1994, p. 7). Unlike virtually any other virus, HIV has the capability of existing in the cell's genome in the latent state so that a substantial amount of the virus is in a form that cannot be recognized by the immune system. Actually we now know that the term "latent" is not quite correct. HIV is constantly reproducing; it never stops. But because it hides within the cells' DNA (covertly copying itself every time the cell divides), it remains undetected. Thus the misnomer "latent" is still used in AIDS terminology.
Quoted from: http://www.teenaids.org/Educators/Facts Research/tabid/71/Default.aspx

Chapter 16

Christ's Physical Corporate Body

In Christ we who are many form one body, and each member belongs to all the others (Romans 12:5).

MADE UP OF SONS OF GOD

The passage of Scripture above is so powerful. It describes our role and function as sons of God. When the Body of Jesus Christ truly becomes one with this revelation, true sonship will be manifested on the earth. Christ is the Head of the Church. We are the Body of Christ. At the Last Supper, the Passover feast, Jesus said to His disciples, *"This is My body broken for you."* (See Luke 22:19.) That statement was made manifest when His own physical body was broken and spilled out on the cross so that He could give birth to a new Body called the Church (sons of God). He sacrificed His body so that *He could put us on!*

Jesus took upon Himself the dead bodies of a sinful world and brought to life a people called the Body of Christ. The *body* He took upon Himself—*a body you prepared for me* (see Heb. 10:5), formed in the belly of Mary—was destined to die. That body took on sin and death and was shed and left in the grave. Then, He gave Himself a new body formed out of the very blood and water that poured out of His side (His womb). This Body He called the Church, destined to eternal life. He left Himself on the earth in His Body called the Church (that is established on the revelation that He is the Messiah, the Son of the living God) because He needed to continue to operate in the world in a spiritual as well as physical sense, even as He walked the earth before.

Today He is filling up the parts of His body with the lives of men and women who would understand that their bodies belong to Him and give them up as an offering. He is doing this by the indwelling Holy Spirit consuming those bodies and ushering them into His perfect will.

The Body of Christ must embrace the fullness of being a "body." Not just a body of believers gathering to worship or to confer, but a body with each member belonging to first and foremost the Head (Christ) and then to each other, all functioning for the benefit of each other.

The following diagram is meant to give a visual aspect to the inner workings of the Body of Christ.

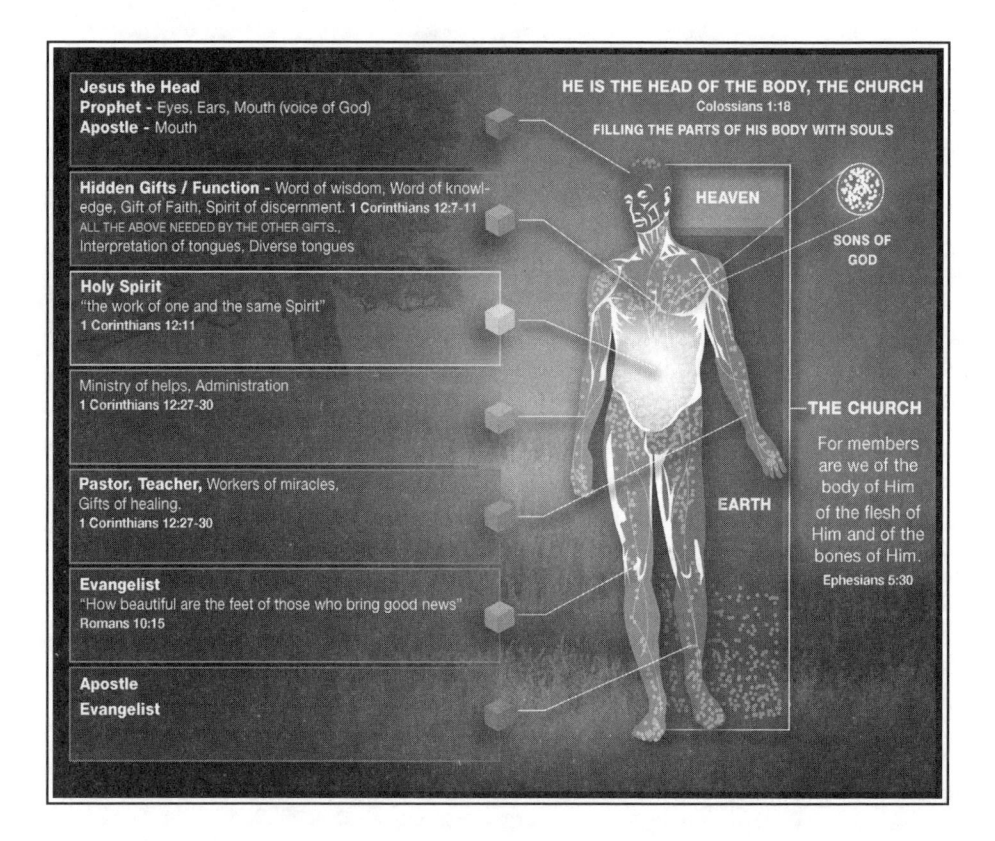

Jesus the Head
Prophet - Eyes, Ears, Mouth (voice of God)
Apostle - Mouth

Hidden Gifts / Function - Word of wisdom, Word of knowledge, Gift of Faith, Spirit of discernment. 1 Corinthians 12:7-11
ALL THE ABOVE NEEDED BY THE OTHER GIFTS.,
Interpretation of tongues, Diverse tongues

Holy Spirit
"the work of one and the same Spirit"
1 Corinthians 12:11

Ministry of helps, Administration
1 Corinthians 12:27-30

Pastor, Teacher, Workers of miracles,
Gifts of healing.
1 Corinthians 12:27-30

Evangelist
"How beautiful are the feet of those who bring good news"
Romans 10:15

Apostle
Evangelist

HE IS THE HEAD OF THE BODY, THE CHURCH
Colossians 1:18
FILLING THE PARTS OF HIS BODY WITH SOULS

HEAVEN

SONS OF GOD

THE CHURCH
For members are we of the body of Him of the flesh of Him and of the bones of Him.
Ephesians 5:30

EARTH

A careful look at this diagram will reveal that every member of the Body must function in his or her role in order for the fullness of the Head (Christ) to be revealed on the earth. Although there are gifts, there is still *one* Holy Spirit, and with Him present within each member then at any time as the Holy Spirit deems necessary, a member can operate in any of them. Every member is so vital to the effectiveness of the Body that any member weakened in any way dilutes the power and capacity, capability and effectiveness of the Body.

It is so amazing that when any damage is caused to the physical body, every member, cell, blood vessel, and tissue is immediately placed on alert; a message is sent to the brain that something is wrong; the necessary diagnosis is given as well as the corrective measures; all actions are concentrated on that damaged area to bring healing and restore wellness. (See Galatians 6:1.)

Similarly, as members of the Body of Christ, our approach must never be one of "as for me and my house," but rather, if a member stubs a toe, then the rest of the Body should have a headache and thrust into action to bring relief. As believers most of us came into an environment of competition and jostling for position, and unaware, most of us end up doing the same thing. That is a false picture of the true Body of Christ. The true Body takes the stand that *"we who are many form one body, and each member belongs to the others"* (Ephesians 5:30).

Chapter 17

The Mystery of the Communion

*The cup of blessing which we bless, is it not a partaking of the blood of Christ? The bread which we break, is it not a partaking of the body of Christ? Because **we, the many, are one bread, one body, for we all partake of the one bread*** (1 Corinthians 10:16-17 Literal Translation).

How Do We Relate or Commune With Each Other?

God is a God of intimate relationship! God who sits enthroned above the circle of the earth, who laughs at the ignorance of mankind, got so involved and intertwined in the affairs of man that He gave Himself up as a sacrifice to secure His eternal relationship with us. And yet, He does not expect anything from us that He has not done Himself, setting an example for us to follow.

That is why the Scripture declares in Ephesians 5:1-2, *"Therefore be imitators of God [copy Him and follow His example], as well-beloved children [imitate their father]. And walk in love, [esteeming and delighting in one another] as*

Christ loved us and gave Himself up for us, a slain offering and sacrifice to God [for you, so that it became] a sweet fragrance" (AMP).

The key to the fulfillment of this Scripture and our relationship with God according to His design is found in the mystery of the communion. Where there is no genuine relationship between believers, there can be no real communion or partaking of the body and blood of Jesus Christ.

Communion With Christ and Each Other

Relationship is the core of communion with Christ and with each other. God's design for this level of relationship began in Leviticus 24:5-7, which says, *"Take fine flour and bake twelve loaves of bread, using two-tenths of an ephah for each loaf. Set them in two rows, six in each row on the table of pure gold before the Lord. Along each row put some pure incense as a memorial portion to represent the bread and to be an offering made to the Lord by fire."*

This Scripture has some powerful symbolism. Let us take a closer look at the message hidden in this verse. This bread was called the "Bread of His Presence" and only the High Priest, Aaron, and his sons were allowed to eat of it. It was to be a lasting covenant on behalf of the Israelites. The instruction given to Moses for the priest was really a type of the broken body of Christ; it brings together a wholesome Body called the Church that operates in unity and agreement. As a result it sends up to God an aroma of the purity in which the Body operates and relates to Him and to each other.

Twelve loaves all having the same amount of ingredients speaks to us of cohesiveness and freshness and points to the selection of twelve disciples, the first manifestation of the Body of Jesus Christ.

Two rows (side-by-side) speaks to us of unity and points to Jesus sending His disciples out two by two, walking in agreement. This type of agreement is manifested as unity of purpose and not uniformity.

Incense speaks to us of purity in our relationships with God and with each other, going up to God as a sweet-smelling aroma—a sweet and memorial sacrifice.

Years later as Jesus is about to fulfill His purpose on earth and release upon the earth a new breed of people called the Body of Christ (also known as the Church), He makes this statement in Matthew 26:26-27: "*While they were eating, Jesus took bread, gave thanks and broke it, and gave it to his disciples, saying, 'Take and eat; this is my body.' Then he took the cup, gave thanks and offered it to them, saying, 'Drink from it, all of you.'*"

Jesus blessed the loaves, which represented His body. The word *bless* denotes "speaking well of." When the subject is God, His speaking *is* His action, for God's speaking and action are the same thing. When God is said to bless us, He acts for our good, seeing what we need most and not what we deserve (the cross is the primary example).

When we bless each other, we express good wishes. When we bless as Christ did the loaves and fishes, when He miraculously multiplied them, and as He did the memorial bread (communion) and the infants, *we consecrate them for divine use*. The word *consecrate* is defined as "to declare to set apart as holy or sacred, to dedicate something to a specific purpose."

In other words, as Jesus blessed the loaves representing His body, He was consecrating them as His Body before the Father for divine use. And so anyone who partakes of His Body has been consecrated to divine use. In John 17:19 Jesus says, "*For their sakes I sanctify (to make holy, purify, consecrate) myself, that they also might be sanctified through the truth.*" Then He lifted up the cup of wine and gave thanks to the Father. The word *thanks* (*eucharisteo*)[1] speaks of "to be grateful, to express gratitude."

Why was He so grateful? Hebrews 12:2 answers that question: "Looking to the Author and Finisher of (our) faith, Jesus, who for the joy set before Him endured (the) cross" (Literal Translation). The word *joy* comes from the root word *grace* and is defined as "to rejoice, exuberant joy, gladness of heart."

Jesus gave thanks for the shedding of His blood because the blood was the guarantee of His Body being consecrated for divine use.

In 1 Corinthians 10:16-17, Paul reemphasizes the hidden message in Leviticus 24 and Matthew 26 when he stated, "*The cup of blessing which we bless, is it not the communion of the blood of Christ? The bread which we break, is it not the communion of the body of Christ? For we, the many, are one bread, one body, for we all partake of the one bread.*"

The word *partaking*[2] comes from the root word *koinonos*[3] and speaks of "partaking (i.e., literally participation or intercourse, communion)."

The word *one*[4] speaks of one numerically—as in one person and not one in essence and different in personality, but as one person.

The word *bread*[5] speaks of "a loaf."

The word *body*[6] speaks of "the body as a sound whole."

When we consider all the above definitions, we boldly embrace the truth that Jesus' physical body is represented on the earth as His Church. Although the Church is made up of many parts, she is indeed one *body* or one *loaf*. Not one in essence but different in personality, but one as in "one person." Partaking of the communion is actually intercourse with each other—the mystery of becoming one with Him and each other, every time we eat His body and drink His blood. In context with communion the word *intercourse* is not unlike the word *know* in Hebrew. The word *know is* an intimate word. It is the same word used to refer to a man knowing a woman sexually. As believers we are asked to know the Godhead at this same degree of intimacy. The question here is, what really is sexual intercourse? Isn't it two bodies becoming one? What really is intercourse? Isn't it the joining of two to become one? Jesus' prayer in John 17 was that we will be one with each other just as He is one with the Father. What exactly did He mean? He is in the Father and the Father is in Him. How much closer can one become? That is the meaning of intercourse. Generally our relationship as believers with each other has been shallow, because we have never fully embraced the *cause* of Christ by having intercourse with each other as He has with His Father—becoming one with Him and with each other through the mystery of partaking in His body and blood with the understanding.

His blood is the *Life* that fits every bone, ligament, and joint together and the very *life* in the bone marrow of His physical Body (the Church). His blood becomes the very breath of His Spirit that protects our spiritual bone marrow, keeping it free from contamination. (See Eph. 4:1-16.) In speaking of the blood, there would be no presence of the Holy Spirit within the believer without the presence of the blood of Jesus. In the natural the life of any living body is in the blood. In a spiritual sense the Spirit flows in the blood, which is protected by the bones. There would not be any redemption of sin without the blood. Therefore our spiritual bone marrow (the framework on which our transformed nature is established) must be strong enough to sustain us as a people as we grow up into Him (Christ), who is the Head. From Him the whole Body, joined and held together by every ligament, grows and builds itself up in love, as each part does it work, until we all reach unity in the faith and in the knowledge of the Son of God and become mature, attaining to the whole measure of the fullness of Christ. (See Ephesians 4:16.) As Jesus' Body we are also bone from His bone and flesh from His flesh (or bone of His bone and flesh of His flesh). Therefore our spiritual bones must carry within them the presence of the Spirit of God to the degree that was manifested in the life of the prophet Elisha. When his physical body decayed, his bones were left as a witness to those around of the power and presence of God in which he operated.

Bones are defined as the most durable part of the human body and used to describe deep feelings or affection. In Genesis 29:14, when Laban met Jacob, he said these words to him: "*Surely you are my bone and my flesh*" (Literal Translation).

These are the same words Adam spoke to Eve: "*You are bone from my bone and flesh from my flesh (original language).*" (See Genesis 2:23.) When the Scriptures speak of bones, they are referred to as something of substance, life, and strength. Bones protect the inheritance of future generations as proof of ancestry. Emotional pain does not affect the skin (flesh) of a person, but is felt in the core of the body, which is the bones. That is why unforgiveness can and has caused arthritis and other bone diseases.

As we have been saying, we are Jesus' bone from His bone and flesh from His flesh. When our spiritual bones are dysfunctional, it cripples the rest of the body. The bones are the framework and the foundation on which the body stands, just as the rock forms the foundation on which a house is built. The psalmist David and the apostle Paul called Jesus the "*solid rock of our salvation,*" and the "*chief cornerstone.*" In the physical body, bones function to move, support, and protect various organs in the body. Bones produce red and white blood cells. Marrow, nerves, blood vessels, and cartilage are found in the bones. In spiritual terms, Christ's bone from His bone (the Church) is His identity (His witness) in the earth (the framework on which He is established). Hidden within His bone are the very treasures of His blood and of His power as were displayed in the bones of the prophet Elisha. Therefore, the bones must be free from contamination so that the body's framework will remain healthy to carry and display the presence of God within.

This leads to a better understanding of Paul's statement in 1 Corinthians 11:27: *"Therefore, whoever eats the bread or drinks the cup of the Lord in an unworthy manner will be guilty of sinning against the body and blood of the Lord."*

Here is where the mystery is revealed! What does it mean to partake in an unworthy manner?

Let us consider the following:

When we come into the Body of Christ but do not allow ourselves to be "molded into the dough" to become one with Him and the rest of the Body, we partake of it in an unworthy manner.

Being among believers and not fully being sold out to God—but seeking to enjoy the benefits of being a believer—is partaking in an unworthy manner and is also guilty of sinning against the body and blood of Jesus Christ.

This is not about eating and drinking of the symbolic bread and wine, whether or not we partake of the physical emblems. It is really about our attitudes toward the Lord and His Body (believers). It is really about our heart following after fellowship and communion with Him and His people that really counts and determines whether our manner is worthy or not, whether we are guilty of sinning against His body and blood.

The verse continues, *"For whenever you eat this bread and drink this cup, you proclaim the Lord's death until he comes"* (1 Cor. 11:26).

The power of partaking of the communion, which is really communion with God and each other in a wholesome and wholehearted manner, is that it declares to principalities and powers that Jesus died to make us *one new man*. And the reality is it cannot be tampered with.

Interpersonal Relationships

This is where interpersonal relationships in the Body of Christ can be handled differently if we embrace the truth of this verse. Paul ensures that we do not miss the power of the message by laying it even heavier on us, *"For anyone who eats and drinks without recognizing the body of the Lord eats and drinks judgment on himself"* (1 Cor. 11:29).

Where there is greed or selfishness in operation, we are partaking of the Lord's Body in an unworthy manner.

When we treat each other as outcasts, quarrel and slander, speak or think ill of each other, we are partaking of the Lord's body and blood in an unworthy manner, not discerning or recognizing His Body.

When we as members of the Body of Christ do nothing to enhance our relationship with the Lord to strengthen the Body, then we partake of the body of Christ unworthily.

Understanding Divine Connections on the Journey

We must understand that on the journey God has strategically given us to each other. His desire is that we will discover the different aspects of Himself within each other, causing us to grow and mature from His presence flowing from within us. Therefore if our relationships with each other are purely for personal gain and gratification and we do not recognize that they must be based on having a relationship with Jesus Himself, so that the relationship will reflect our attitude and fellowship with Him, then we are opening ourselves up to judgment simply because we fail to recognize the body of the Lord.

When the Bread of His Presence in Leviticus 24 was to be baked before being placed before the Lord, the bread had to be baked with a specific amount of flour and incense in order to meet the requirement acceptable to the Lord. Many times in our relationships, we do not know how much of our involvement is needed to give the relationship the cohesiveness that is necessary to cause it to mature.

It is vitally important in our encounters with the Body of Christ on the journey that we know when to be God's instrument and when to allow God to be God in the relationship. When we are coaching someone in their relationship with God, and when we are being coached ourselves by someone else, we must be careful not to attach ourselves too closely. We must be discerning about this so that when the time comes for a change in season to connect with another member of the Body of Christ, both parties will have matured enough to accept and embrace the change in the new direction the relationship must go—with the understanding, of course, that members of the Body of Christ can never cease being a part of each other.

In essence every relationship that is really being "molded into the dough" at every stage of the journey in God must be allowed to come together by the Spirit of the Lord. On the journey, every connection the Spirit of God allows in our lives is to cause us and the other individual to be molded at another level in the dough, until every believer becomes one with Him and as a result we become one with each other. Then there will be no separation between the dough and the bread itself. (See Romans 12:5—every member belongs to all the others.)

Why Are Some Weak and Sick and Some Have Died?

A chain is as strong as its weakest link! When relationships have not come about according to God's prescribed manner, the end result produces weakness in these relationships that eventually affects the Body as a whole. It leaves behind sicknesses such as jealousy, bitterness, misunderstanding, misinterpretations, and suspicion, and these eventually result in spiritual death. Fleshly, soulish relationships must not be allowed to operate in the Body of Christ.

One of the dangers of forming relationships without the direction of the Holy Spirit is the inability to discern whether the individual is part of the "true loaf" or someone who treats it with contempt. In 1 Corinthians 11:19 we read, *"There must be also heresies among you, that they which are approved may be made manifest among you"* (KJV). In the next chapter, we read, *"If one part suffers, every part suffers with it; if one part is honored, every part rejoices with it. Now you are the body of Christ, and each one of you is a part of it"* (1 Corinthians 12:26-27).

The Ultimate Communion

In Matthew 26:29, Jesus concludes His speech to His disciples with these words, *"But I say to you, I will not at all drink of this fruit of the vine after this until that day when I drink it new with you in the kingdom of My Father"* (Literal Translation).

The word *new* in this verse means "to renew, to dedicate, consecrate into qualitatively new use, freshness."

The word *fruit* speaks of "offspring—generation, produce, from the root meaning procreate, figuratively: to regenerate, be born, bring forth, conceive (diversity, kindred, nations)." From another root word meaning: generate, to become (come into being).

In other words, Jesus is saying to His disciples (and by extension His Body): "I will not drink of this fruit, the fruit that will be regenerated, until that fruit is consecrated into qualitatively new use becoming *one new man* with the very divine nature of God, filling every member and every part." Every time we partake of His body and blood with full understanding, it allows the blood of Jesus to bring the many parts or members of the Body of Christ into *one new man*, pointing to the day when indeed the King of kings and the Lord of lords will once again drink the fruit of the vine with this one new man (His Bride) on the great day called the Marriage Feast of the Lamb.

This is indeed the mystery of the communion. It is a communion so powerful that it creates one new man, Jews and Gentiles alike manifesting the very nature and character of Jesus Christ Himself, revealed as the Body of Jesus Christ (the Church). It is a communion that has been set aside for divine use and cannot be tampered with. It is a communion that produces fruit with the power to reproduce and bring forth sons of God for God. This encounter is a must on the journey! You would not want to miss it!

ENDNOTES

1. *Lexical Aid to the New Testament,* from *The Hebrew Greek Key Study Bible, from King James Version* (Chattanooga, TN: AMG International Inc. D/B/A Publishers, 1991), #2168.
2. Ibid., #2842.
3. Ibid., #2844.
4. Ibid., #1520.
5. Ibid., #740.
6. Ibid., #4983.

Chapter 18

The Marketplace

INTRODUCTION

Our most important encounter is our connection with the Body of Jesus Christ. When we have understood how to relate to each other, then our aroma will filter outward to the wider world. A nation is as strong as the families that sustain it, and the world is made up of nations. The Church (a community of nations) is the womb of the nation. If there are factions and divisions among us, then that is the kind of world we will give birth to. We have been so inward-looking for so long that we have lost our flavor for a little while. The family of God is one family, bone of His bone and blood of His blood. There is only one blood type flowing through all of our veins—the redeeming blood of the Lamb.

As a family we are expected to reflect the glory of our Father, which is His nature and character, His love, His justice, His mercy, His righteousness, His wisdom, His light, His truth. All the attributes of *Abba* must be seen in His offspring. Jesus said it this way, *"All men will know that you are my disciples, if you love one another"* (John 13:35). So as we are presented to the world as "one loaf," our Father has prepared lots of "divine encounters" in the marketplace to be introduced to His Son in the person of His sons manifesting true sonship.

As we are shifted from a Church-only mentality to a more balanced Kingdom focus and reality, it is vitally important to understand those encounters and how to relate to the culture surrounding them as "agents of change" and not as religious freaks. From the opening chapter of this book, we have been progressing through a preparation of knowing and understanding who we are and whose we are. We were made aware of our birthright or inheritance and the covenant promise God has made with us, His offspring. Understanding came to open our eyes to the magnitude of the presence of the Holy Spirit within us, and His one and only desire is to inhabit our bodies as His temples as He reconnects us to our Source, Jesus. He is the one who waits with bated breath to introduce us to *Abba* as sons, so that the fullness of the manifestation of the heart of *Abba* for His creation will be unveiled to the world—a world of people curious to find God on their own terms, a God they do not know, yet deep within desire to know.

Every level of the preparation process points to the fullness of the manifestation of the sons of God coming forth as agents of change, answering to the groaning of creation, and drawing them toward the journey to the marketplace. For all of us, we came from the marketplace ignorant of God's great inheritance in us and us in Him. Now that we have gained an understanding of who we are, we must be reintroduced to the marketplace as sons of God (both genders), walking and fulfilling His mandate to restore and reconcile all things to Himself. There is an urgent call to the marketplace, and we as sons of God must answer the call.

Our reintroduction to the marketplace is an embracing of the same environment we were previously a part of. Embracing simply means to understand that regardless of what that environment represents, the reward of Jesus' suffering is to reconcile all things to Himself (see Col. 1:15). As agents of change our purpose is to understand our role and assignment as given by the Holy Spirit with regard to where He will position us at different times on the journey in the marketplace. We are to understand the sphere of authority we are expected to operate in and how to recognize the spiritual forces at work on our assignment.

The Marketplace

OPERATING AS AN AGENT OF CHANGE

Let's ask ourselves how a son of God operates in the marketplace as an agent of change. Before we can respond to this question, we must first understand that the marketplace is wherever we are and whatever our pursuit in life as occasioned by the Holy Spirit.

A son of God operates in the marketplace as an agent of change by, first of all, being in a place of deep intimacy with the Godhead and answering the loud cries of the marketplace. An agent of change will hear the cries and will be:

- Light in thick darkness.
- Truth where falsehood and deception are present.
- Love in a loveless world.
- Hope in a world of hopelessness and despair.
- Joy in a world where laughter is swiftly disappearing.
- Life to the dying (spiritually, emotionally, and physically).
- Salt to preserve truth, love, and hope so as to preserve a legacy for the next generation.
- Wisdom where the wisdom and worldly counsel of man becomes futile and can no longer give the strategic answers needed.
- Peace where there is so much restlessness that the silent cry is *Stop this train and please let me off*, in the midst of turmoil and adverse circumstances, where stress and pressures result in premature deaths and suicides.
- Righteousness to uphold the standards of God where unrighteousness is prevalent.
- Justice and equity where injustice and inequality exist.
- Integrity and good stewardship where compromise and dishonesty are displayed, restoring dignity where it is lacking.

In essence we must first embrace the fullness of intimacy available within the God in us, where His Kingdom is established, and then wrap our arms around the marketplace. Embrace the marketplace fully. The marketplace is calling!

THE ASSIGNMENT

What exactly is the assignment of the agent of change? For every believer God has designated a particular assignment. That assignment is really the part of God He desires to manifest through His sons, so that He can be seen, known, and correctly interpreted. Every believer must be in the place where the fullness of the assignment can be realized. The believer must know the vision of God for the assignment, so as to avoid any deviations from it. With the vision God releases a newfound language, called the language of God. It is filled with the wisdom and truth of Heaven and stands in full agreement with the heart of the Father. The language of God must not be mistaken as religious jargon, but rather the believer must avoid anything that will cause compromise with regard to truth, righteousness, justice, or anything that would distract us from the vision of God. That might be pressure, adverse circumstances, or any other such thing. The reality that must be settled and embraced is that even as God reveals the vision, He also gives the strategy.

In times past, we believed that our assignment was to go into all the world and preach the Gospel. That assignment is known as the commission mandate. We were taught to tell someone about Jesus through our words and not necessarily by our lifestyle. But there is another mandate that is far greater than the commission mandate. That mandate was God's original design for His sons when He first released man's commissioning and assignment. The dominion mandate is found in Genesis 1:26 and it says, *"Be fruitful and multiply and subdue the earth."* In Genesis 1:28 God blessed them and said to them, *"Be fruitful and increase or multiply in number; fill the earth and subdue it. Rule over the fish of the sea and the birds of the air and over every living creature that moves on the ground."*

This mandate not only encourages us to preach the Gospel but it also speaks to a seed within the very DNA of our being with the power to multiply and increase, bringing forth after our own kind. God's original intent was that as He poured into Adam (man) the fullness of who He is (Father, Son, and Holy Spirit), the fullness of His image and likeness, His nature and character, man—being filled with God—could only bring forth the same seed. In this way, there would be a multiplication of the very life and nature of God present on the earth through the seed of Adam. Sin came and forfeited the manifestation of the fullness of the life and nature of God in mankind for a season until the Christ appeared and once and for all fulfilled the dominion mandate in Genesis 1:26 and Genesis 1:28. He then left His sons in the earth through a Body called the Church (a community of nations or an assembly of peoples) to continue the multiplication of Himself in the earth through them. This is the mandate the sons of God will take to the marketplace.

God has restored all things. Some have already been manifested and there are others yet to be fully experienced in this hour, but the restoration of the dominion mandate was not only restored on the cross but manifested immediately. It is important to note at this point that the dominion mandate was not given to believers or Christians. It was given to a son (Adam). *Adam* means "man" and *Eve* means "life-giver"; therefore the command was given to a life-giving man.

The seed of the Godhead manifested in Christ was not released into believers or a group of people called Christians. Neither one of these groups can reproduce the seed of the Father, because neither group carries the seed of the Father. The seed is in the genes, and only sons (both genders) can have the transference of the seed that will bring forth the genetic image and likeness of the Father. Remember, the heart of this book is the journey to "sonship," and there is no other identification.

As we continue to explore the journey in the marketplace, let us remember that the heart of the message is for a son who has submitted to the preparation process as discussed in all the sections of this book. With that in mind we will continue by discussing our role and assignment in the marketplace.

Chapter 19

Our Role and Assignment in the Marketplace

The sons of this age (the world) *are shrewder and more prudent and wiser in [relation to] their own generation [to their own age and kind] than are the sons of light* (those who profess to know Him) (Luke 16:8 AMP).

OUR ROLE IN THE MARKETPLACE

The word *role* speaks of "an actor's part, one's task and function. The part a person or thing plays in a specific situation or operation." The word *assignee*, as a noun, speaks of "a person who has been given the right or duty of acting in a place of another." The phrase *to be assigned* means "to allot persons, to nominate, to appoint to a position." The word *assignment* speaks of "the thing or task assigned." So what is our role?

As agents of change (knowing who we are), we understand that we have been given the right and duty to act in place of another and that "another" is Jesus. That then is our role. We are the representative of Jesus as a "son." As His agent we have been appointed to a particular position, and that position is our assignment, the capacity in which we will function. We have the responsibility to ensure that we are correctly and strategically positioned.

It is very important to note that an assignment has a time frame built into it. An assignment might be short-term or long-term. The assignment may change, and this is solely dependent on the one giving the assignment. Our role, however, never changes, regardless of the assignment. Our role is who we have become. If this is not clearly understood, we may find ourselves in an assignment that is obsolete, causing us to become powerless to operate or function and ineffective in bringing about change. Murmuring and complaining is the evidence of a feeling of powerlessness. We become miserable and disgruntled. Complaining is the language of defeat when one feels powerless to change the circumstances.

Ask yourself the following questions to ensure that you are strategically positioned:

- Do you know that you are on an assignment?
- Do you understand the assignment?
- Do you relate to where you are currently positioned as a job, a place only for earning income? Or as a place where divine purpose can be realized?
- Are you passionate about your current position?
- Do you feel fulfilled in your current position?

If you have identified your position as an assignment, you should also seek the heart of God for His vision for the assignment.

Let us clarify the word *vision* right here. It is defined as "the act of seeing or the ability to see a picture formed in the mind or heart." The Webster dictionary defines a *visionary* (the person) as "someone who imagines how things should be and pays little regard to how things actually are or are likely in fact to be." This echoes the Father's vision as He gives Jesus the reward of His suffering by reconciling all things to Himself, regardless of how things appear in the natural.

In other words, when we know our assignment and are given the vision, we are unmoved by the physical manifestations around us, and we are operating solely under the reality of the truth of the manifestation of the will of God, which will be done on earth according to His will in Heaven. That is our only reality!

THE STRATEGY FOR THE ASSIGNMENT

After we have understood the assignment and the vision, the next step is to be given the strategy. The words *strategy* or *strategic* are military terms; they speak of "skill, management, position, considerations, movement." In relation to war, they speak to "the conduct of the campaigns and choice of operations to be attempted, and tactics." The word *tact* and *tactical* are very useful words to note. Combined they bring out the following meaning: "an understanding of how to avoid giving offense and how to keep or win goodwill." It sounds like the word *subdue* (get the upper hand of, tame, bring into subjection, soften, make gentle, tone down, colors, effect, mood), which comes from our mandate to *dominate*. (A plan of action astutely thought out as to advance a purpose or gain an advantage.)

It gets even better as we explore the word *astutely*, which has within it a negative and positive connotation. It is defined as "shrewd (intelligent and worldly wise)." It is so important to understand the culture and language of the place where we are positioned in our assignment.

"*Sagacious*, keen and perceptive, having or showing discernment in judgment." For this exercise, we will concentrate on the positive aspect of this definition. As part of our strategy, in addition to being tactful or using tact, we become God's intelligence and wisdom revealed to the unbeliever, operating from God's perspective with keen discernment as we seek to understand the culture and language of our area of assignment. It must not be said of us as it was said of the people called the chosen ones (the Jews) of Jesus' time. When compared with the parable of the shrewd manager in Luke chapter 16, Jesus made a profound statement. He was speaking about how the shrewd manager was asked to give up his position and immediately began to create a reserve for himself. His master praised him for being shrewd and prudent. In verse 8 Jesus said these words, "*The sons of this age (the world) are shrewder and more prudent and wiser in [relation to] their own generation [to their own age and kind] than are the sons of light (those who profess to know Him)*" (AMP).

Understanding this and having a strategy ensures success in your assignment. If you are currently in a specific position in the marketplace but you are not sure if that is your assignment, now is a good time to ask yourself a few pertinent questions:

- Has God been speaking to you about preparing yourself for your assignment (maybe going back to school)?
- Are you too afraid to start something new?
- Are you afraid of change?
- Do you think that you are unqualified?
- Where is your confidence level?
- Are you in the correct assignment?
- Has God been speaking to you about starting your own business?

Perhaps your assignment might be to look after your children. Regardless, being in the wrong assignment or having no assignment brings no glory to God. We cannot fully represent Him in the marketplace and fill our roles as agents of change unless we address some of these questions. Here is a good place to stop and ponder awhile.

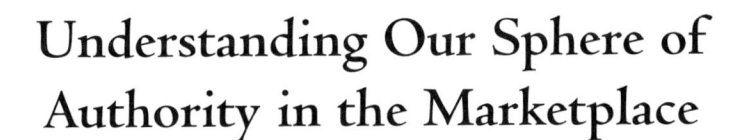

Chapter 20

Understanding Our Sphere of Authority in the Marketplace

It has pleased [the Father], that all the divine fullness (the sum total of all the divine perfection, powers and attributes) should dwell in Him permanently. And God purposed that through (by the service, the intervention of) Him [the Son] (Jesus) all things should be completely reconciled back to Himself, whether on earth or in heaven, as through Him, [the Father] made peace by means of the blood of His (Jesus) cross (Colossians 1:19-20 AMP).

Understanding Our Sphere of Authority

Philippians 1:9-11 states, *"This I pray: that your love may abound yet more and more and extend to its fullest development in knowledge and all keen insight [that your love may display itself in greater depth of acquaintance and more comprehensive discernment]"* (AMP).

God will reveal Himself to us to the extent of our love for Him. The deeper our love for Him goes, the wider it extends to each other and the greater our understanding and discernment of God and the things of God. The key then is love, because God is love Himself. True authority operates where love is present.

To explore this subject of understanding our sphere of authority, we must first define the word *authority*. It is defined as "power, right, to enforce obedience (or the right to command and to be obeyed). To have or exercise authority over; delegated power (give, receive or act, to do, personal influence)." We cannot exercise authority unless we have been given authority.

The first criterion in understanding authority is to know "who we are," and the second criterion is to know the source of our authority. Always remember that respect is something that is earned but authority is given. It is important to note that all authority comes from God, as stated in Colossians 1:15-16: *"He (Jesus) is the image of the invisible God, the firstborn over all creation. For by him all things were created: things in heaven and on earth, visible and invisible, whether thrones or powers or rulers or authorities; all things were created by him and for him."*

Many times we forget this passage of Scripture and even have the notion that things are happening outside the control and divine will of Heaven. Every single event in world history works in accordance with the divine will of Heaven. Heaven has purpose on earth for everything. Pharaoh, for example, was created with one divine purpose—to cause God to manifest Himself at the Red Sea for His glory and His glory alone. Colossians 1:15-16 extends itself in verses 19-20, *"It has pleased [the Father] that all the divine fullness (the sum total of all the divine perfection, powers, and attributes) should dwell in Him permanently. And God purposed that through (by the service, the intervention of) Him [the Son] all things should be completely reconciled back to Himself, whether on earth or in heaven, as through Him, [the Father] made peace by means of the blood of His (Jesus) cross"* (AMP).

This is explosive. In verses 15-16 it was made clear that all things were created by Christ and for Christ. After sin ravished creation, the Father made peace with creation through the blood of His Son on the cross. By that same cross, it pleases the Father that all things should be completely reconciled back to Christ. Therefore there is absolutely nothing that is outside of the reconciling arm of God—that is key to understanding when on assignment in the marketplace.

God is and will always be the ultimate authority on earth and in Heaven according to Scripture. Any authority exercised on the earth then is delegated authority. Nothing takes place on the face of the earth unless God allows it. Any authority that has been assigned to the believer on the earth has been delegated by God. So the believer's ultimate authority is God.

In the spirit as well as in the natural, a person cannot delegate authority to another if that person has not been given the authority to do so, or if that person fails to operate in or exercise the authority he or she has been given. If a person is unable to exercise the authority given in its fullness in every area that has been assigned to him or her, then that person is really powerless to delegate or exercise delegated authority outside the sphere of authority given. As mentioned before, we must understand our assignment and the heart of God (His vision, will, and purpose) for the assignment before we can understand our sphere of authority. Regardless of the situation or atmosphere we operate in, the heart of God must be clearly understood and fully embraced if the assignment is to be fulfilled.

In the natural when we are assigned our positions in the workplace, it is considered unwise to try to step outside of the boundaries laid out for us. If we attempt to do so, it would be termed out of place and could even result in termination or transfer to another post. One of the reasons for this is that we would not have been privy to the integral discussions and decisions undertaken by those given the authority to operate in the area. We would find ourselves speaking about things or trying to handle situations that are way outside our scope. We would be operating outside of the sphere of authority we have been given. This is very important to understand as we journey to the marketplace. As was said earlier, God will give us the vision as well as the strategy to function in our assignment.

As part of the strategy, God has given us tools and assigned to us a specific area in the realm of the spirit, that He has given us authority over, as well as the support we need to exercise that authority. He never sends us on an assignment without giving us the spiritual authority to function in that assignment. That is why we must know and understand our assignment and ensure that we are operating within the sphere of authority outlined for us in the realm of the spirit. The problem with most of us is that we are unaware or ignorant of the boundaries within which we are assigned to function.

When Jesus sent out the disciples in Matthew 28:18-20, He said these words to them: *"All authority in heaven and on earth has been given to me (delegated by the Father to me). Therefore go and make disciples of all nations, baptizing them in the name of the Father and of the Son and of the Holy Spirit, and teaching them to obey everything I have commanded you."*

Let us examine this Scripture in order to get a greater understanding of the heart of Jesus in conveying this message. The original Greek relating to this verse reads this way: *"Having gone, then disciple all nations (race, tribe, people), baptizing them into the name of the Father and of the Son and of the Holy Spirit, teaching them to observe all things whatever I command you."* In other words, Jesus was saying, "Go make sons that will allow Me to establish My kingdom in their hearts." It is also very important at this time to place some emphasis on the meaning of the word *name* in relation to baptizing *into* the *name*. The Strong's Greek translation defines this word as "authority, character, fame, reputation." It gives importance to the confession of the name, or for the sake of the person so confessed. To be baptized into someone's name means to be baptized into the faith or confession of that person and to be identified with the person's character and purpose.

Baptized in His Name

Let's take a closer look at this command to baptize disciples of all nations in the Name of the Father, Son, and Holy Spirit.

When Jesus revealed or made the Name of the Father known, He did it by demonstrating the nature and character of the Father as reflected in His own life. His words were, "If you see me, you have seen the Father. I and the Father are one." (See John 14:9.)

Jesus fulfilled the will of the Father by what He did and said while on the earth. He said this in John 17:1-5:

> *Father, the time has come. Glorify your Son, that your Son may glorify you. For you granted him authority over all people that he might give eternal life to all those you have given him. Now this is eternal life: that they may know you, the only true God, and Jesus Christ, whom you have sent.* **I have brought you glory on earth by completing the work you gave me to do.** *And now, Father, glorify me in your presence with the glory I had with you before the world began.*

When we as sons of God are baptized, it is not only a baptism of repentance (a leaving behind of the old things and publicly declaring our confession of Christ), but we are baptized *into His Name*. This means that we are baptized into His fame, His reputation, His character, His suffering, His burial, His resurrection, and into partaking in the fullness of His person, into becoming Him in the earth. We become one with Him even as He and the Father are one.

Jesus' prayer in John 17 makes this clear. He prays, *"Holy Father protect them by the power of your Name—the Name you gave me, so that they may be one as we are one"* (John 17:11).

He continues in verse 21:

"Father, just as you are in me and I am in you. May they also be in us so that the world may believe that you have sent me. I have given them the glory that you gave me, that they may be one as we are one: I in them and you in me. May they be brought to complete unity to let the world know that you sent me."

Baptizing the nations therefore speaks of this same baptism. As the sons of God go to the nations, the entire structures of the nations—not just their people, but their systems, laws, and policies—must be baptized *into the name* of the Father, Son, and Holy Spirit. His Name, not just teachings about Him, but His character, His nature, must leave an indelible mark on the nations and their people. The will of God must be displayed with a declaration that the Kingdom of God has come! That was the command and He gave it to sons, not to Christians. That is the mandate given to us in operating in our sphere of authority in the marketplace. This is the command and posture that defines our position in the spirit realm.

With this understanding in mind, we can then take up the mantle of Jesus' command in Mark 16:17. After giving them the commission, Jesus said these words:

These signs will accompany those who believe: In my name they will drive out demons; they will speak in new tongues; they will pick up snakes with their hands; and when they drink deadly poison, it will not hurt them at all; they will place their hands on sick people, and they will get well.

Not having a comprehensive understanding of our mandate has caused us to believe that the things mentioned in this verse will be manifested only in a natural sense, but there is another dimension to this verse. Let us examine it more closely. What we are about to reveal in this verse is key to avoiding the subtleties of the enemy to entrap and prevent us from accomplishing our assignments as we operate in the marketplace.

Driving Out Demons

We do not fight against flesh and blood (see Eph. 6:12), so there are demons all around us doing satan's dirty work. At this point we will not discuss rank and mode of operation, acknowledging the fact that demonic forces are very active in the atmosphere around us. The authority released for the command to "drive out demons" extends to the ones that will manifest very subtly in the atmosphere of our assignment, impersonating the personality and activities of the people and systems in which we must function.

Speaking in New Tongues

There is a tongue, a language in the Spirit that causes demonic forces to flee. There are tongues that are given at the point of being baptized in the Spirit, but intimacy with the Holy Spirit will release another level of tongues capable of disarming, confusing, and scattering the enemy from the realm of the assignment we have been given to function in.

Picking Up Snakes With Their Hands

Snakes represent deception, cunning, and subtlety. Hands represent strength, power, might, and cleanliness. We will expose and not be blinded by the deception that operates in the area of our assignment. Paul confirms this in Ephesians 5:6 by making this statement: *"Let no one deceive you with empty words."* Verse 11, *"Have nothing to do with the fruitless deeds of darkness, but expose them."* Verses 13-14, *"But everything exposed by the light becomes visible, for it is light that makes everything visible."* Verses 15-16 say, *"Be careful then how you live—not as unwise but as wise, making the most of every opportunity, because the days are evil."*

Understanding and walking in a place where we can embrace our authority gives us the power to discern and resist the deceptions around us.

Drinking Deadly Poison and It Will Not Hurt Them

The word *poison* is defined as "a substance that when absorbed by a living organism kills or injures it (slowly or cumulative by repeated doses), harmful influence or principle. To inject with, corrupt, pervert, fill with prejudice, spoil, person, mind." The demonstration of our authority in this area is that we will be surrounded by poisons of all kinds and yet not be infected or tarnished.

Laying Hands on the Sick and They Will Get Well

In our area of assignment, there are all kinds of sick persons (emotionally, psychologically, physically) around us; people just simply messed up, all covered up in clothing of degrees, makeup, walls, and partitions. These individuals can and will be easily misunderstood if spiritual discernment, godly counsel, and wisdom are not present. We have been given the authority to unmask the lie within and bring healing and wholeness.

Reverse Strategy!

As a result of the believer's lack of understanding of sonship and the authority given to him or her, the reverse has taken place. Demonic powers have taken advantage of believers and rendered them impotent. Poison has entered their system and caused injury. That is evident in their behavior. They have been rendered confused in their actual identity, and they buckle under the pressures that are forcing them to conform to the system they were sent to influence.

Instead of laying on of hands, the believers become sick themselves with pressures and stresses, releasing all kinds of unwanted chemicals into their systems, causing strokes and heart disease and other kinds of physical and emotional imbalances. Their families suffer in the process. It is important to note that the enemy does not have respect for the believer, only the God that is present within the believer. Unless the believer has made the transition from a believer to a son, the power of God resident within the believer that gives the confidence to exercise the authority needed on a daily basis remains dormant.

The authority that is released to access the spirit realm can only operate in the spirit realm; therefore the believer who seeks to enter that realm without real legal access as a son will find himself or herself in a war that he or she will be unable to combat successfully. The believer, in this instance, is operating outside of the sphere of authority given.

Let me echo some of the things mentioned in earlier chapters. The first assignment the believer has is to have full authority over himself or herself. Specifically, we are to understand that we are, first and foremost, spirit and not to be controlled and governed by the sinful nature resident on the inside. The sinful nature has no power where love is present, and true authority operates where love is. Our mandate is to reflect the love of Jesus as we partake of Love Himself.

Believers have engaged an enemy they sometimes perceive to be powerless, and as a result have been defeated. The enemy, on the other hand, has taken time to study the life of the believer at length and understands every weakness. The enemy is not powerless, but the power resident within the believer is greater. *It is all-powerful!* As sons, we must be in a position to declare as Jesus did, "The prince of this world is coming and has no hold on me." The believer then must be convinced that the love of God is very present and must enter into and operate in that love. Until the believer can access the power of that love, then he or she remains exposed to the powers that be.

Chapter 21

Know What Controls the Area of Your Assignment in the Marketplace

We are not unaware of his [the enemy's] *schemes* (2 Corinthians 2:11).

KNOW WHAT CONTROLS THE AREA OF YOUR ASSIGNMENT

As an agents of change, we must understand that in the working environment there are unseen forces that influence policies, and these affect, in turn, management decisions at all levels. In most cases these policies appear to be legitimate, since it is projected as being in the best interest of the advancement of the organization. All are encouraged to embrace these unseen influences for the betterment of all.

Taking a closer look at these policies with eyes of discernment, it is interesting to note that in most cases the welfare of the most important assets in the organization, the employees, is not always really high on the list of priorities. In most cases the employee becomes another statistic and the driving force for the advancement of the organization. The employee in some cases is highly rewarded materially, but at a high price to his or her physical and mental health. The skill of the employee is needed as long as the employee produces at maximum capacity. Someone said it this way: "They drive you and then they ride you." Let us keep in mind here that all of this is influenced by unseen forces.

Satan is still the prince of the power of the air. He still has power and influence in the systems of the world. Where he is given legal access, he will strive. Legal access is given wherever there is an open door in a life that has the character traits of the enemy. In most cases that life or lives are unaware of the open doors. The believer is not exempt. Remember also that the Kingdom of God operates wherever the will of God is done, and we are carriers of the Kingdom of God. Therefore as we function in the marketplace as sons, the fulfillment of our assignment will release the Kingdom of God wherever we go.

Negative Character Traits Operate in the Marketplace

What are these character traits operating in the marketplace?

- Lack of true identity, which causes people to step on others to make a name for themselves and gain perceived acceptance.

- Lack of identity is a product of fear: fear of failure, fear of people, and fear for the future (holding on and refusing to pass on anything—knowledge, goodwill, investing time—to another person.)

- Manipulation. One of the deadliest and most subtle character traits in the marketplace. It reveals itself through control, greed, and selfishness. That kind of trait will manifest itself in doing anything for the sake of money, and by doing anything to secure position. This type of insecurity speaks to a personal need for self-preservation and self-gratification.

- Thirst for power. This is the key character flaw of the enemy. This thirst for power is the fruit of pride and shows itself in self-exaltation.

- Exploitation. It is displayed through dishonesty and issues of integrity.

Wherever these traits are present in a life or lives, the enemy has an open door to exercise influence. The result of these unseen forces and influences, seen in behavioral patterns, is manifested in the government and leadership of the organization. The same top-down principle holds whether resulting in good or evil. It flows from the head down.

The agent of change must be aware of some of the ways in which these influences affect the employee in the workplace:

- Deadlines that produce pressures resulting in tension, stress, and eventual death if left unchecked.
- Life dedicated to the organization, leaving no quality time for self or family and hardly any time for God.
- Uncertainty and restlessness.
- Failed marriages and broken homes.
- Physical, emotional, and psychological problems resulting in bad eating habits.
- Lack of physical exercise, and poor health.
- Suicides at the corporate level when uncalculated changes occur.

I must reiterate here that it is at times like these that a son of God operating in the marketplace as an agent of change must be aware of his or her assignment. The danger of entanglement in the very system we were called to influence is great.

The apostle Paul said to the Corinthian church in 2 Corinthians 2:11, "*We* [Paul and his companions] *are not unaware of the enemy schemes.*" Unfortunately for most of us we have been unaware until now. We can get trapped in the atmosphere created by the culture of the organization, and accept these things as the norm. In some cases being busy gives some of us a sense of self-importance. For others busyness is another way of shutting out the noise within our beings. Unless we are made aware of these things, we are powerless to discern the different demands that are made on us and others, and unable to respond correctly. It is incumbent upon the agent of change to be aware of the influences that control the area of his or her assignment.

Once again the key for the believer to function in the capacity of an agent of change is that he or she must be free from the character traits of the enemy and be correctly positioned to exercise godly authority over the things that control the area of his or her assignment. He or she must carry authority that is not characterized by loudness or self-assertion, but love, peace, joy, righteousness, justice, mercy, and compassion with much wisdom and discernment. It does not preach at people or carry a judgmental attitude, but exercises patience and operates in divine timing. It must be the kind of authority that releases the aroma of Heaven, as we are clothed with Christ as our inner garment and display His presence within us as His outer garment.

Unseen Forces

For a brief moment, we will address some of the actual unseen forces that govern the character traits displayed in the marketplace. Ephesians 6:10 states, *"Be strong in the Lord [be empowered through your union with Him]; draw your strength from Him [that strength which His boundless might provides]."* The *Amplified* version of verse 12 continues, *"We are not wrestling with flesh and blood [contending only with physical opponents], but against the despotisms, which are tyrannical conduct* (subject to no one). *Master spirits operating in the world, which are rulers and authorities* (those in decision making positions, positions of influence)." These are manifested in the physical through the government of the organization. We should also note that the spirits of wickedness in heavenly places control territories and regions.

Second Corinthians 10:3-6 states:

> *Walking in flesh, we do not wage war according to the flesh. For the weapons of our warfare are not fleshly, but powerful in God to casting (demolishing) down strongholds, pulling down imaginations, and every high thing lifting up (itself) against the knowledge of God and bringing into captivity every thought into the obedience of Christ and having readiness to avenge all disobedience, whenever your obedience is fulfilled* (Literal Translation).

Most believers would agree that they have read these Scriptures and tried to put them into action. The problem is that for too long believers have engaged the enemy in all kinds of warfare that has accomplished nothing other than muster frustration for the believer and expose his or her weaknesses and shallowness. The intention of this book is to help bring the believer into a place of maturity as sons and by so doing empower him or her to resist and overcome these challenges.

We said earlier to be strong in the Lord and in His mighty power (see Eph. 6:10). God never leaves the believer exposed; any exposure is the believer's responsibility. In addition to giving us our assignments, He will give us the necessary weapons to take care of all the negative influences we will encounter. This is not a time to run from the marketplace. We are mandated to face and embrace the marketplace as agents of change and ambassadors of reconciliation. This is important not only because a greater portion of our time is spent interacting with the marketplace, but also because we are the only hope, light, truth, integrity, and reality of Jesus that the marketplace will ever see and experience.

Weapons of Warfare

As sons of God, there is innate within us some of the most powerful arsenals the world will ever encounter:

- We have within us the *strength* and *power* of the all-powerful God. We have the power to stand up under any situation and, having done all the situation demands, to continue to stand.

- Because truth is resident on the inside of us, we can stand firmly in truth, in our innermost parts as God desires, and in any situation where falsehood is prevalent.

- We can stand in integrity and moral rectitude (correctness, moral uprightness) and righteousness.

- We have the Prince of Peace, our Shalom resident indeed within us. Therefore we can and must stand as agents of peace, having firm-footed stability, and be in a position of promptness and readiness produced by the good news that reveals the truth of the Gospel made manifest by an experiential relationship with the Word of God coming forth from within us. Our peace is tangible and no one can take it from us. Our lives are cemented in the blood of Jesus, and our place of intimacy with God creates fear in the heart of the enemy.

- Since faith is resident within us, we have complete dependence and trust in the God of faith on the inside of us. That understanding enables us to stay in agreement with the vision of Heaven for our assignment and not to be governed by what we see or hear.
- The Word of God is God Himself, so as we become one with the Word, the enemy must respect the power of the Word coming forth from within us even though he has no respect for us. He must respect the God within us when we allow God to display Himself in and through us.

There are others weapons such as those what Paul described in Ephesians 6:5: *"Servants (slaves), be obedient to those who are your physical masters, having respect for them and eager concern to please them, in singleness of motive and with all your heart, as [service] to Christ [Himself]"* (AMP). We often equate our service in the church as service to Christ, yet in the workplace where the need for Him to be made manifest through our lives is greater, we do not apply the same principle, forgetting that we are co-laborers with Christ, for He prepared the assignment (this good work) before the foundation of the world.

Ephesians 5:11 says, "Take no part in and have no fellowship with the fruitless deeds and enterprises of darkness, but instead [let your lives be so in contrast as to] expose and reprove and convict them" (AMP). This speaks of consistency in lifestyle—a great weapon. Our atmosphere should always be one of truth. There must be agreement between what we speak and the atmosphere within us.

In Ephesians 5:13, we read, "When anything is exposed and reproved by light, it is made visible and clear" (AMP). This speaks of truth that releases light where there are no unresolved issues in our own lives. Nothing is hidden.

And what about conversation? Daniel refused to eat the food of the Gentiles. Make sure to stick to vegetables and drinking water. By that I mean we must stick to our own diet (conversation seasoned with salt and pleasing to the ear; the ear of the Holy Spirit within us), lean as it appears. The life of the truth of God coming forth from within us produces life, and life gives life. Do not partake of the worldly diet (conversation) of the ones God gave to us to influence.

The most powerful weapon is to know the will of God and walk in it. That is the believer's greatest form of fulfillment, confidence, assurance, and power. (See Colossians 1:9.) Knowing and understanding sonship will enable us to walk in high levels of discernment that give us access to the angels assigned to us for our specific tasks.

The greatest weapon of all is intimacy. As the greater power within us is activated through intimacy and is reflected in our lifestyles, it releases a strong message in the Spirit that declares: "This one has been with Jesus."

As we conclude this chapter, remember that we cannot exercise authority beyond the place of our own experience in God. We cannot speak to anything that is still in operation within us. Darkness cannot resist light and fear cannot resist love. Confusion cannot withstand or conquer perfect peace. So go forth as a son of God and be an agent of change, an ambassador of reconciliation, and operate in your sphere of authority. Rise above what controls the area of your assignment and embrace the marketplace!

From My Heart to Yours

Throughout the pages of this book, I have had one objective in mind. That is to enable you, the reader, to be equipped with the necessary tools to become the fullness of the full measure of all the fullness of Christ, hidden within you. My prayer is that the Holy Spirit will give to you the Spirit of wisdom and revelation so that you may know Him better. I pray that your eyes will be enlightened in order that you may know the hope to which you have been called, Christ *in* you, the Hope of glory.

Someone is going to ascend to the heavens and sit in the very being of the Father. Someone is going to be the very essence of the glory of the Father in the earth. Someone is going to be the very heartbeat of *Abba*, releasing His fragrance wherever he or she goes. Someone is going to give Jesus the reward of His suffering! Why not you? Why not now?

So be strong in the Lord and in the power of His might, and let us together as a Body take hold and possess our inheritance as sons of God and sons of the Kingdom. The child (the immature believer) must indeed become a "son."

It is truly time to possess your inheritance; the earth is groaning for your manifestation as a son!

For unto us a child is born, unto us a Son is given—given to a dying and chaotic world, a world that awaits "sons" (both men and women) of God to bring life and light in the face of death and confusion. So go forth and possess; go forth and become; go forth and be a son! And remember to enjoy the journey!

CONTACT THE AUTHOR

Lydia Newton

C/O Kingdom Restore Inc.
No. 8 West Road, Clermont
St. Michael, Barbados

Tel: 1 (246) 232-5682

info@kingdomrestore.org
www.kingdomrestore.org

Additional copies of this book and other book titles from DESTINY IMAGE™ EUROPE are available at your local bookstore.

We are adding new titles every month!

To view our complete catalog online, visit us at:
www.eurodestinyimage.com

Send a request for a catalog to:

Destiny Image™ Europe

Via Acquacorrente, 6
65123 - Pescara - ITALY
Tel. +39 085 4716623 - Fax +39 085 9431270

"Changing the world, one book at a time."

Are you an author?

Do you have a today, God-given message?

CONTACT US

We will be happy to review your manuscript
for the possibility of publication:

publisher@eurodestinyimage.com
http://www.eurodestinyimage.com/pages/AuthorsAppForm.htm